Virtual Vernacular

Virtual Vernacular

Sarah Bonser

CRC Press is an imprint of the
Taylor & Francis Group, an **informa** business

CRC Press
Taylor & Francis Group
6000 Broken Sound Parkway NW, Suite 300
Boca Raton, FL 33487-2742

Printed on acid-free paper

International Standard Book Number-13: 978-0-367-00219-0 (paperback)
978-0-367-00223-7 (hardback)

Visit the Taylor & Francis Web site at
http://www.taylorandfrancis.com

and the CRC Press Web site at
http://www.crcpress.com

This book is dedicated to my incredibly supportive family.
I am so grateful for the patience, love, and
optimism you all share with me.

Contents

Part IV
Character

Acknowledgments

I have been incredibly fortunate to have been afforded this opportunity. Thank you to the CRC Press team, Sean Connelly for reaching out to me and being incredibly supportive and informative. Thank you to Shreya Agrawal for your excellent editing and attention to detail. Thank you to Chris Totten for being an amazing resource and source of inspiration for this new author. I am exceptionally lucky to have received editing help from Jeffrey Anderson, Evan Chakroff, and Madeleine Hahn. You are incredibly talented and I am so thankful for your expertise.

I am grateful that the Game Developers Conference (GDC) Advisory Board saw potential in this line of research and documentation. Clint Hocking worked with me to help translate and distill incredibly specific knowledge into something that's usable across disciplines. Thanks to Chris Chinn for explaining how portals work and sharing his experience going from architecture to game design and Gabe Newell for getting me in contact with him. Thank you to Chris Carney and Doug Cook North as well for sharing some insight on transitioning between architecture and game design.

Thank you to the faculty and staff at Knowlton School of Architecture, especially Lisa Tilder, Stephen Turk, Jackie Gargus, Doug Graf, Jeffrey Kipnis, Rob Livesey, and Bart Overly. Each fostered an expectation that entertainment mediums possess design value worth studying.

My unique perspective is afforded by colleagues who were patient and kind enough to explain "why" when asked a question. Thank you to Michael McLaughlin, Christopher Keener, Emily Neymeyer, Chris Bruzzese, Matthias Olt, Peng Liew, and Nandita Kamath.

None of this would be possible without my friends and family. Steven Biersteker constantly inspires me and pushes me to do so much more than I knew I was capable of. Thank you to Bill and Jayne Biersteker for your support and encouragement. Thank you to Thomas and Sheila Bonser, Mary and Tony Bonser, and Marie and Corey Cottrell for being with me every step of the way to becoming an architect. Thank you for your constant support, it means the world to me.

About the Author

Sarah Bonser is an Architect, licensed in the State of Washington, with a focus on residential architecture. Her work has primarily been mid-rise and high-rise construction with an emphasis on the documentation of design. She is an advocate for technology improving empathy for design goals and reducing barriers to contribute to the design process. Bonser has developed construction documents paired with isometric line drawings to help with decision-making and construction. Bonser primarily focuses on the integration of new technologies into workflows, ensuring their usefulness and a low barrier for entry throughout the project's life cycle. Her research on opportunities for technology in architecture has spanned from Virtual Reality to 3D Laser Scanning. Her work on Building Information Modeling (BIM) workflow and the advancement of digital documentation tools has been cited in *Beyond BIM: Architecture Information Modeling.*

Bonser studied architecture at The Ohio State University. She earned a bachelor's degree in Architecture with a minor in City Regional Planning and continued there to earn her master's degree in Architecture. Her independent work focuses on architecture playing the role of a teacher or a narrator. Her thesis work focused on conveying architectural concepts to a general audience with the help of technology. She has spoken at the Game Developers Conference (GDC 19) on the topic of World Building with Architecture.

Introduction

This book will primarily reference architecture that holds design paramount. "Architecture" separates itself from "buildings" through intentionality; whether it draws from local inspiration (Vernacular) or academic sources (Canon). Similarly, it will also reference games that already hold their environments responsible for storytelling. Not every game uses its environment to tell the story; not every building holds its design concept paramount. That being said, opportunity for design can emerge anywhere.

Please also note that this book begins with big design ideas and transitions to small design ideas. This correlates to a typical design cycle for architecture. In order to mitigate the uncertainty associated with creative problem solving, architectural design at firms is broken into three phases, followed by a documentation phase. Feasibility or Concept Design identifies the goals of the building and a variety of ways to achieve them.

The client agrees to a development strategy. This reduces the redesign costs as the architect can start to narrow down possibilities. Schematic design sets up a system for successfully meeting the goals defined in the feasibility study. The client buys off on the strategy and the team moves into Design Development. Architects will typically fully coordinate a design and supply "alternatives" as branched designs before committing them to the main model. This allows the team to always have a safe "default." It also ensures that a solution that requires mutually exclusive systems isn't assumed to be "working." Once the optimal branches are committed to the main model, the architect begins the Construction Documentation process. This chases down literally how each detail should come together to ensure that each dimension affords the design proposed. This creates fewer changes from option to option as the project moves forward. Introducing large changes late in design derails precise coordination efforts from earlier in the design process.

Theoretical implications and conceptual interpretations of overarching concepts are identified in concept and schematic phases. Applications of concepts are sorted out during development and resolved in documentation. Redirection on major ideas should be handled with extreme care as they become more costly in later phases. An expertly executed concept that is poorly communicated to a team will read as incomplete or misguided. Identifying these concepts and trusting that the direction chosen for the project is appropriate is at times hard, but pays off. Using details as a follow-through on major concepts can contribute to a more memorable experience.

As an author with limited experiences in the grand scope of this profession, I will supply this caveat: This book is written from the perspective of an architect trained in theory (BS and MArch) and Registered Architect in the state of Washington.[1] I live and work in the United States and primarily use imperial feet and inches. For a few years, I worked on projects in India and Dubai and had the luxury of working in metric units. Most firms still use some AutoCAD aided by SketchUp. Our new industry standard for designing and documenting is Revit. This almost certainly affects the design of the buildings.

I will be referring to work that has been constructed as "Built Architecture." Architecture designed for a game or entertainment environment will be referred to as "Virtual Architecture," as it is not responsible for but may opt in to real-world constraints such as feasibility, constructability, or safety.

It is incredibly important to recognize that by current statistics, my profession is not currently diverse and has been less so historically. National Council of Architectural Registration Boards (NCARB)'s 2018 report indicates 2% of licensed US architects are black, 1% are Latino, 9% are Asian. For reference, in 2018 the United States had an ethnic makeup of 12.8% black, 16.3% Latino, and 4.8% Asian. Architecture as a profession has many barriers to entry. When I refer to architecture as something that represents a culture, the hope is that it is constantly getting better at representing more members of that culture.

[1] Only licensed professionals can use the title "Architect." As the software industry has taken some liberties with the title of architect, I will similarly drop this nomenclature. Many great designers that I'll be referring to in this book are not licensed. In the event that it matters, I'll use the title "Registered Architect."

Part I

Concept

Understanding how real-world forces impact built architecture can help create new relationships for fictional architecture in fictional worlds. Architecture often acts as a sponge for all of the inherent forces inflicted on a location, population, or culture. Great architecture can convey this while gracefully addressing constraints of constructability, feasibility, and safety.

Many parties are required to build a structure, at the very least—an owner, a contractor, and an architect. It is in the best interest of all parties to complete a building that is constructible, feasible, and safe. The general contractor checks the drawings for constructability and will make changes as necessary while building it. The client will work with the architect throughout the design to ensure that the building remains feasible to fund. The architect will work with engineers, permit reviewers, and inspectors to ensure that the building is safe. If not, the municipality will hold the certificate of occupancy until requirements are met. These checks create a shared responsibility for the welfare of the building.

Constraints are primarily where built and virtual architecture differs. All of the parties involved have an impact on how the building ends up looking. It is not purely a design exercise.

Virtual architecture can opt into these visual constraints for storytelling purposes, but these are certainly not responsible for them in the same way. Virtual architecture has a good deal more authorship related to the design of a building, supposing which constraints to hold the building accountable for as opposed to an inevitable rule requiring it. Textures that inevitably adorn built structures as a result of clips or seams in materials become chosen for virtual architecture.

Architectural design can improve immersion and can direct interest. Game design currently pulls from architecture through the lens of other entertainment industries. "Vernacular" categorizes works that are influenced by local forces more than aesthetics. Many game environments could be categorized as such due to the impacts of gameplay and entertainment on their design.

Games as a medium have a unique opportunity to create fictitious "first-hand" experiences. It can open a new perspective to a player.

> *By seeing something through the eyes of a character, the player works to bridge the gap between the virtual and literal experience.*

While many trades contribute to this experience, this book will focus on architecture specifically. Academics and critics hold architecture responsible for things like sustained conveyance of a concept: a visualization for the geopolitical state of a culture, biography of an owner, manifesto of an architect, the character of a neighborhood. It's easy enough to copy a design precisely, and to be honest, there is certainly enough source material to appear as unique. As games are becoming more sophisticated, improving photorealism will result in diminishing returns from a storytelling perspective. Architecture designed for a different location, time, and purpose will inevitably feel lacking. As each building is created uniquely, replicating the textures that make their way onto built structures leaves some missed opportunities when applied to a new context. To a certain extent, rendering to further fidelity would reasonably have diminishing returns when compared to generating more thoughtful detailing.

Architecture, while at times performs as art, is an engineering endeavor. Describing renderings don't capture the performance and functional qualities of built spaces. Often, summaries and histories of architecture amount to plot summaries that bypass the nuance and understanding. Diagrams are the primary medium of theoretical communication. We focus on how architecture accomplishes the goals that are set up. At its base level, architecture can be described through its materiality, adjacency, light, and scale as shown in the images on the next page.

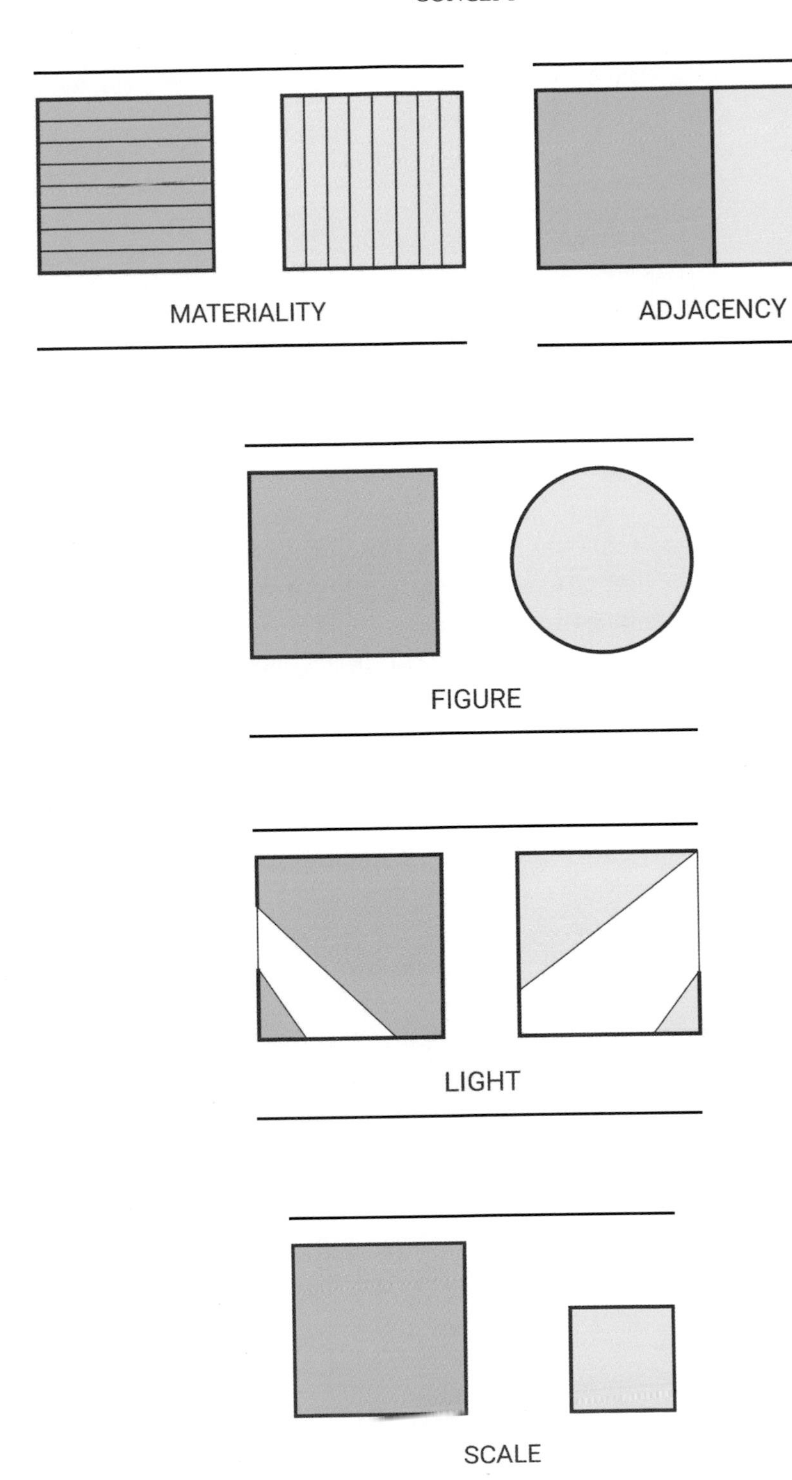
MATERIALITY
ADJACENCY
FIGURE
LIGHT
SCALE

More complex ideas such as proportion and ratio can be extrapolated from "scale" for instance as per the image below.

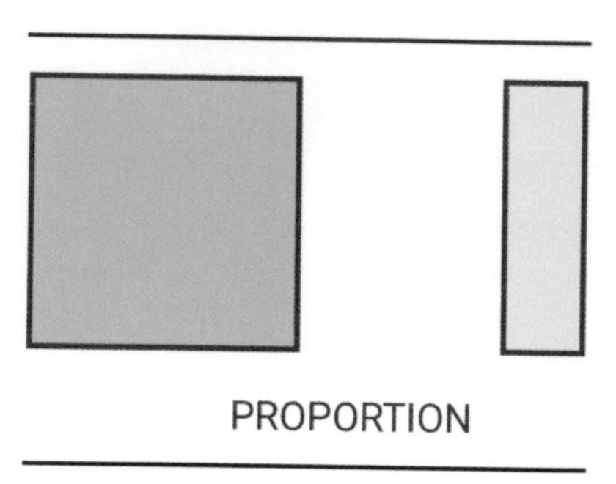

When looking at case studies in this book, comments on architecture will be geared toward the goal of using the tools available to convey a cohesive message. Game environment case studies will follow suit, with the added category of gameplay, with comments geared toward supporting a narrative using the tools available while conveying a cohesive message.

1

Narrative

Expectations for Spatial Design

The elevator pitch of the architecture world is called a *parti* and is conveyed through diagrams. Through perspective alone, it is hard to break down the contributions of any one plane or volume to the feel of a space. Allowing a space to be characterized by proportions, materials, adjacencies, and forms yields a more robust perception. Architecture relies on a variety of relationships to consistently tell a story. This can be as simple as using a taller space to bring more light into the building. It can be as complex as making planes appear to slide apart and carrying that delicate balance throughout the building. Both these instances are shown in the images below.

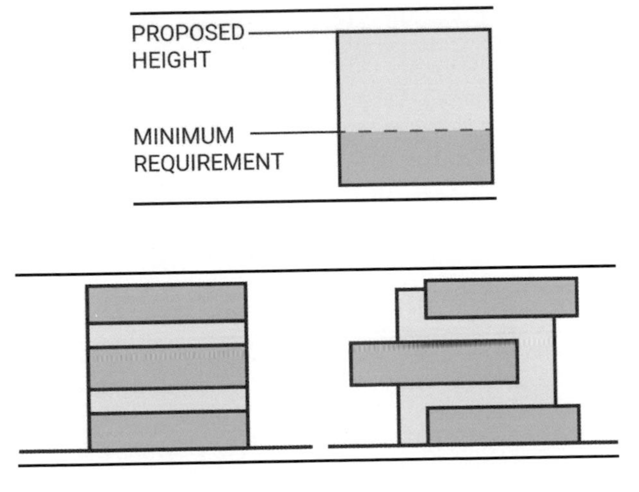

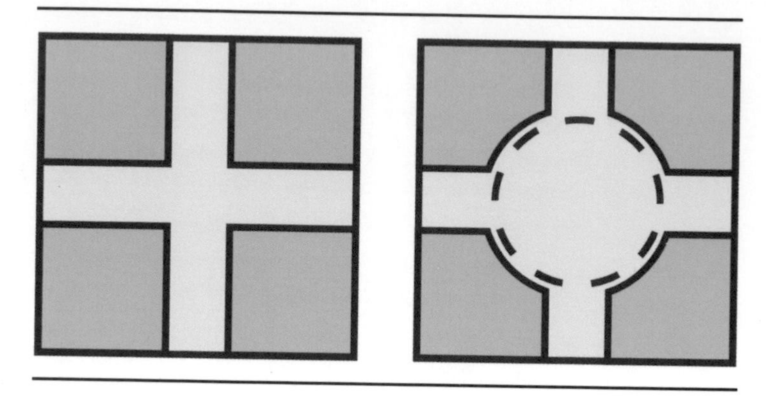

Exciting spaces are available even through straight lines, as long as the architect is clever.

These are primarily worked out in diagrams as small geometry changes in form can have major impacts on the spaces created as shown on the next page. Vetting a wide variety of options using symbolic representation can prevent costly redesign efforts.

As you learn from this book, consider ways to subvert, complicate, simplify, and customize anything you see. Virtual architecture can use built architecture as a springboard to create more fantastic spaces. Pieces of the built environment gently guide occupants every day, identifying and stealing them is an incredibly useful skill to develop.

One of many ways to help players feel engaged in their experience is to create an immersive environment. Games are captivating because they create opportunities for players to interpret meaning from the story and gameplay in a personal way. Giving players the feeling that they're creating a story, despite the existence of storylines and recorded voice lines, is important to memorability and impact.

> *Horror games are incredible at doing this.* Resident Evil 7 *asks the player to move forward and click simultaneously to open a door. All door interactions typically start with a door that the player knows they can interact with. Most games use a triggered animation for a door opening. Resident Evil requires a forward motion to move the door to the open position. While it forgoes the opportunity for an easy transition to a new camera or a full cut scene, it gives the player a feeling of responsibility. This ties the discovery of the area beyond the door with crossing the threshold. These three situations are described in the figures below. This tactic also presents itself as a player is put in a completely compromised situation, using the moment up until death to tell a player how to solve a problem. Treating the tutorial as a last*

ditch attempt is pervasive as the player is realizing the physical limits of the character. Though architecture could play a larger role in the tutorial process, the levels are fantastic at building suspense. Maps are freely provided for areas, confident that the mystery of the spatial layout is not just a one trick pony. The player feels vulnerable in hallways as the niches in hallways present additional blind corners. Long corridors are broken up with props or structure which forces a slower animation as you pass by, also playing into the player's wariness of being in a compromised situation.

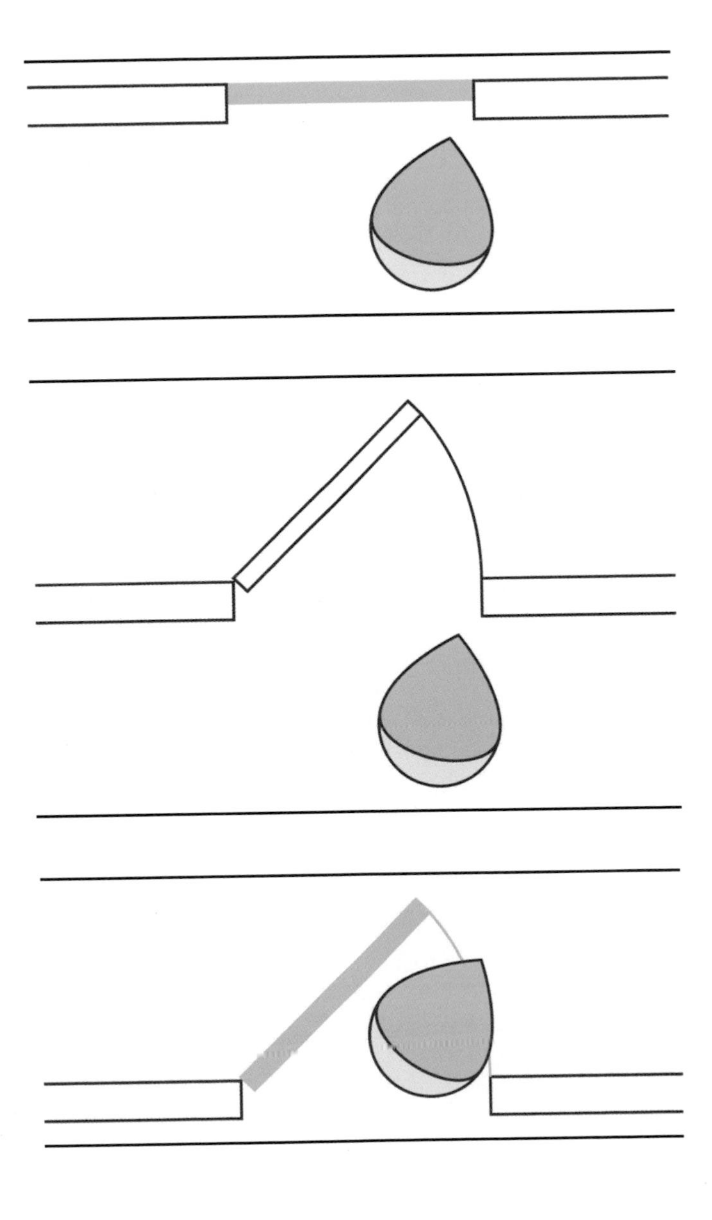

The player finds creativity in the journey, framing, and pacing. The player's experience can float between influencing and being influenced during gameplay. Any control the player gets can be an opportunity for expression. Choices can represent many permutations, and games being a generative medium allow a player to feel responsible and in control of outcomes, resulting in a feeling of accomplishment. Conveying complex concepts and narratives is most simply done in a linear fashion. Games, while certainly the outcomes are predetermined, have interactivity and branching narrative paths. People enjoy playing games for their interactivity. Providing variety to match a player's creativity can be hard as most of everything has been engineered. Designing systems to create the effect of naturally occurring elements is challenging and finite. Videogames as a medium have the capacity to affect players personally, regardless of intellect.

Buildings don't need to respond to every source of influence. Architects will selectively use elements to tell a visual story. These design moves may respond in a variety of ways. Even the lack of response can be a statement.

Comprehension of Spatial Design

Having control over the environment means supplying information to the player intentionally. Developing a system for what a player can be expected to understand about their setting can be helpful as shown in figure below. Put simply, explicit design requires the player to gather information, and inferred

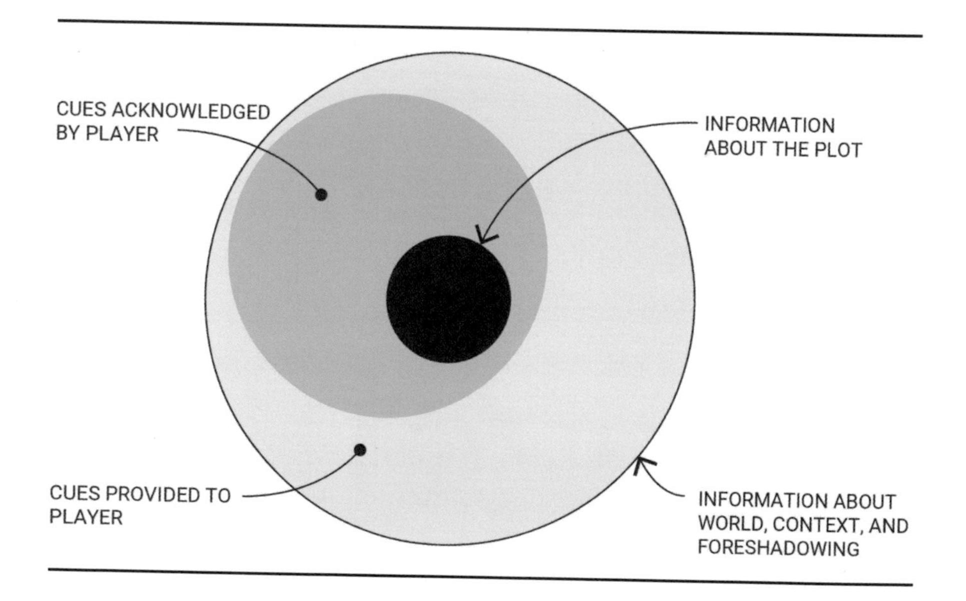

design gives the player information. Explicit design calls for the audience to draw information about complex subjects. You can use it to convey history, social norms, and political climate from the surrounding atmosphere, similar to the way people will learn about a city's culture by traveling there. The urban fabric is heavily influenced by the culture of an area.

> *Most people can recognize the plan of Paris because of one wild policy direction and one person. Haussmann came up with a plan for some avenues, and it took 75 years to carry out. So it was thrown into a different trajectory than how most cities develop, giving it a sense of place.*

Inferred design conveys information passively. This is a quiet suggestion to either push or pull a door based on its handle. Without being tied to a single language, spaces can universally convey a lot of information as shown in the figure below.

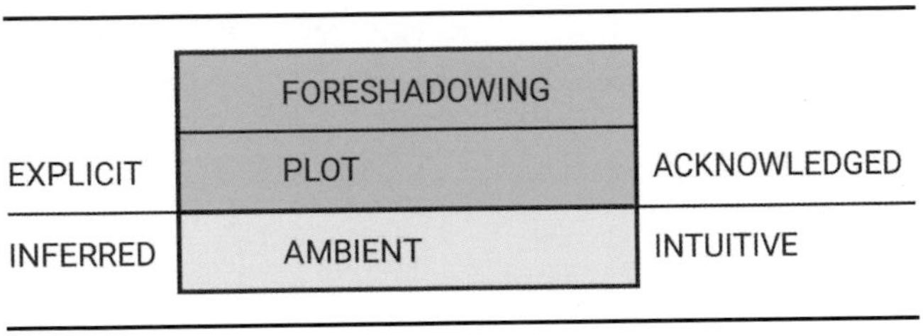

FORESHADOWING
EXPLICIT PLOT ACKNOWLEDGED
INFERRED AMBIENT INTUITIVE

Taking inventory of these cues can lead to a more nuanced understanding of occupant consciousness. Plot should register as above consciousness, as the player needs to have an understanding of why they're providing actions and thoughts toward goals. Once the context is understood, literary moves such as foreshadowing can be leveraged using the environment. Creating effects that register as a coincidence or phenomenon can create an experience below a level of acknowledgment by the occupant.

> *In* Doom II *your character is a paranoid space marine armed with a pistol methodically working his way through a demon stronghold. The environment uses lines and lights to direct you through the level. Soon you'll find yourself pressing up against walls and frantically searching for more supplies. Doom leverages explicit cues to teach the player where to search for supplies using gargoyles and grotesqueries. The later levels appear to have a ritualistic or religious aesthetic to them. Items decorate scenes with strong hierarchical and symmetrical design sensibilities. These indicators prime the player to imagine answers to questions they have about the environment. When monsters spawn or you get dropped into a pit, it can be attributed to any one of the various reasons your brain came up with. This leverages the player's imagination to come up with more convincing reasons than you as a designer could possibly predict for them.*

While each game doesn't necessarily need to reach all demographics, there are some lessons to be learned about designing for a broad range of comprehension levels or for people with a variety of experiences. Demographics are broken into groups in many entertainment industries. Ratings E, T, or M can help designers cater to a ballpark of comprehension levels. While this mitigates the risk of over- or under-explaining plot or character intent in dialogue, it doesn't absolve the conflict entirely. Environments can create a more subtle direction to help the player relate to the world and characters as shown in the figure below. Architecture and space planning can help bridge the gap between telling the player what to do and what the player naturally wants to do.

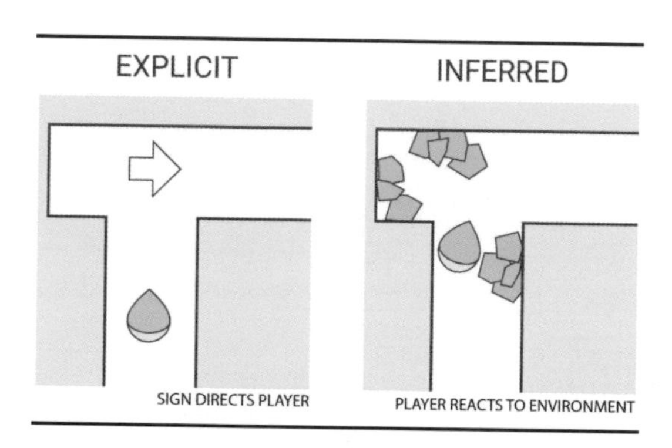

One key aspect to expecting players to process information is to recognize how they are comprehending what is happening. Prioritizing first-hand information (demonstrated to the player) over second-hand information (telling them how to feel) helps players emotionally synch up with their character. Characters and players have different experiences. For instance, in the familiar scenario of a civilian playing as a marine, the player cannot be expected to secure a room like a person with combat training would. In fact, with the combat instincts of the player, the character may struggle to do all of the cool things the story has lined up for them. The level can help or challenge the player selectively and disguise it to not disrupt immersion. This is yet another opportunity for the architecture or layout of the space to assist below the level of comprehension. Many games cleverly integrate learning or tutorial moments into gameplay.

> *Most* Mario *games leverage this throughout the entire game. They teach you how to play the game as if it's a language or piece of music. You learn a jump or power, use it against a few enemies, and right before you get the hang of it, the level introduces a moving platform or another type of enemy. You're given the tools to practice a few times and move on, creating a sense of flow pulling the player through the level.*

Many games leverage sophisticated design patterns. Ico leverages a persistent world of puzzles. Journey uses colonnades and shadowplay as a means of demonstrating distance and speed. *Bioshock* uses public and private spaces to provide players with a feeling of agency in gameplay. Finding ways to intrigue and draw players through the level helps alleviate the feeling of pre-determined destiny.

Architectural design can also integrate wayfinding more seamlessly. Too often, wayfinding is reliant on verbal cues from characters; i.e., a commander tells the character how to get to them, and the character verbalizes something about the environment that the player may not see. Unfortunately, using dialogue to do this requires clever writers and good voice actors if used frequently. It can feel like a crutch when implemented as a reaction to disoriented play testers. Environments can similarly guide players. Even something as simple as developing and maintaining sight lines can diminish HUD or audio orders bossing the player around. Designers can also be prime players with colors, lighting schemes, paint, props, and decals ranging from obvious to subtle. Holding the architecture accountable for setting up the exposition more completely frees up dialogue to take on a tonal role. As a result, emotional moments are much easier to land as they don't have to anticipate a target demographic comprehension level as shown in the figure below.

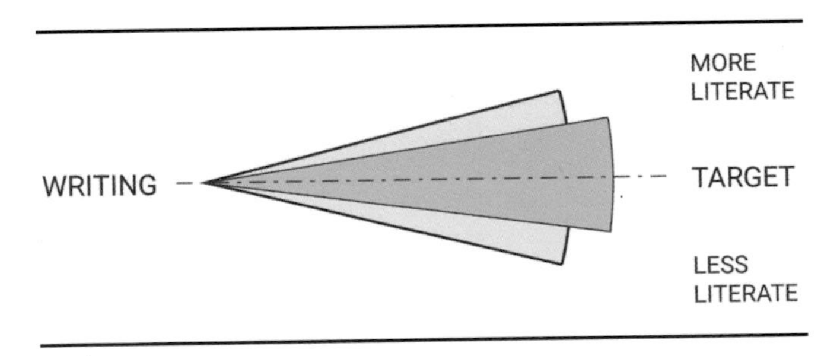

Telling Stories

Architecture is just one of many ways to establish the world that the story is being told in. Relying on the environment like this provides opportunity for smaller characterizing interactions. The convenience of leaning on architecture lies within its function. Architecture allows for interpretation. The shared goals and constraints pose significant changes to the goals of built architecture. Virtual architecture can focus on narrative. Priming the viewer for an outcome can allow actions to take place quickly without losing any audience members. Being mindful of this as a design feature can free up dialogue from justifying character actions in a persistent manner. Assigning a physical location to rising actions and resolutions is a skill honed by movie directors. As the director controls the camera and is actively framing the plot, the design of the space can foreshadow or create drama for an onscreen event.

As with any design language, some tactics work better in one medium than another. In the same vein, you may find that design moves oppose each other. Finding the composition of mediums to borrow from and applications for your design is at times subjective. Objectively, one could evaluate case studies to identify the functionality of specific instances. Given that information, identifying ways to customize it to a new context becomes a much more reasonable task, for instance, the challenge of creating a set amount of functional rooms in an urban level as shown in the figure below. Designers must choose between smaller buildings, inaccessible stories, doors that don't work, overscaled buildings, a system for generating environments, or the most intense burn rate any game has ever seen as shown in the figure on the next page. Certainly this ends up being a combination of a few of those solutions, mixed and matched throughout the game to create variety.

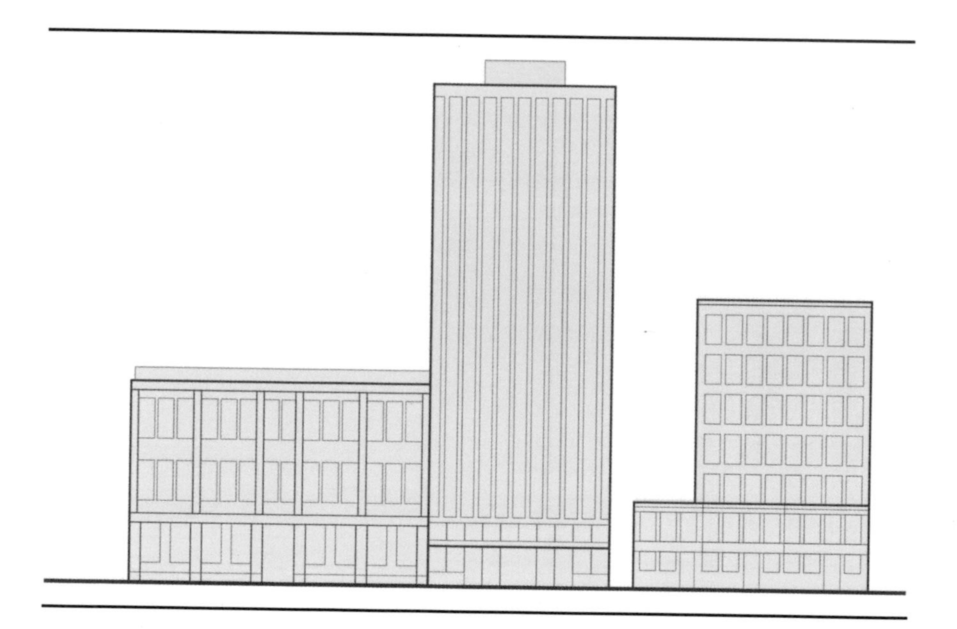

Set design leveraged to immerse the player in lore has been perfected by theme parks and museums. Theme parks are often a network or loop of experiences. Museums tend to be more linear and organized chronologically.

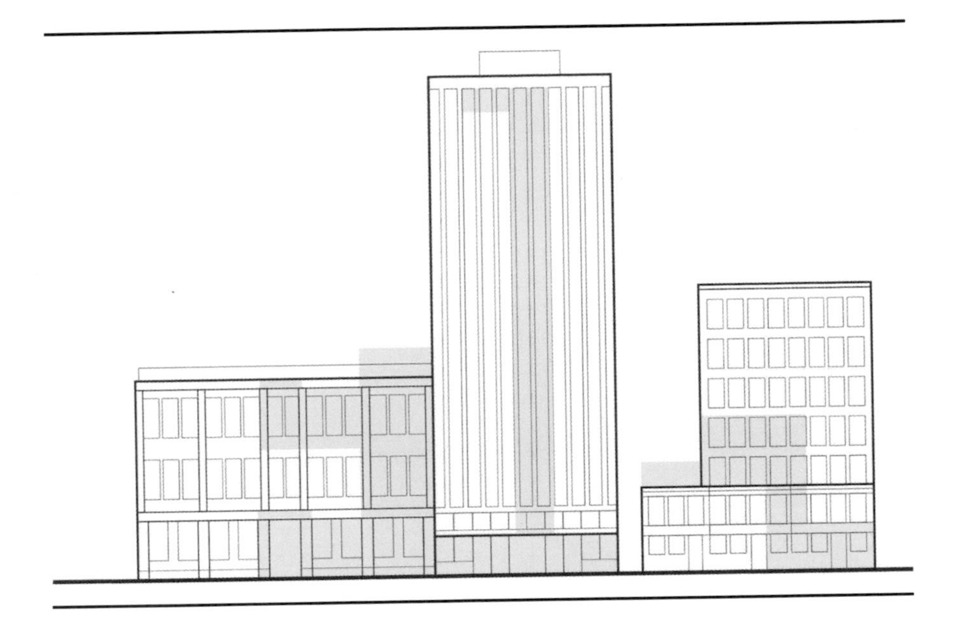

Both manage to create an exciting experience, paced at the occupant's speed. They also suffer from the lack of camera control—while both can rope off certain areas, they still must supply compelling imagery despite limited budget for the scale being portrayed.

> *Disneyland's incredibly popular* "Pirates of the Caribbean" *ride faces multiple challenges. First, it isn't based off of a movie; the attraction gained traction without the help of recognizability and was reliant on the ride alone to captivate audiences. Second, because of its popularity, it had to occupy ride goers through 40–60 minutes of queuing. It couldn't have cast members entertaining the line as it, again, was an original ride. The entry sequence uses sets, props, animatronics, landscaping elements, and music to excite viewers. Exposition is supplied in bits and pieces to create fascination for the riders. Dim lights captivate imaginations and provide a major contrast to the exterior. The dim light helps hide "cracks in the facade", in some ways literally seams in animatronics or mechanics. It also helps reduce overall scope; the designer may choose to render a certain area with more or less resolve. This can afford more complicated design ideas like scale changes. Once the ride begins, the architecture is used to set a reasonable scale for the riders to expect. This allows the out-of-scale features to have more of an effect. The cities change scale as they fade into the background. This created a feeling that more of the world could exist.*

Populating imaginary worlds can at times seem endless. Creating systems to fill in more information becomes much more scalable. When developing narrative, using as many canvases as possible to portray a common theme is important.

Repetition of concept and variety of depiction can make an abstraction of a concept more apparent. Keeping in mind the duration of content, inferred design cues may be more effective than explicit. The expectation for any one piece of the story to do this must scale with the rest of the project as well as the length of time that the story is told over.

Another distinguishing element of good storytelling is pacing. Exposition and pacing has been mastered in novels. *Something Wicked This Way Comes* leverages the prologue to encourage attention to detail and reliance on exposition as the book divulges information. Setting the tone for how information will be conveyed is important for the player. This increased content retention can be achieved by holding architecture to a standard throughout.

There are many applicable architectural studies on narrative as a primary driver. Paper architecture explores the philosophical implications of bold departures from normative spaces. Instant City explores the absolute boundaries for what's required to constitute a city. Walking city supposes a nomadic culture and identifies and pursues key deviation points as a design motivation.

Games that differ in narrative capacity from its predecessors can demonstrate some interesting opportunities. Addressing the pros and cons of different storytelling methods can help optimize comprehension as shown in the figure below.

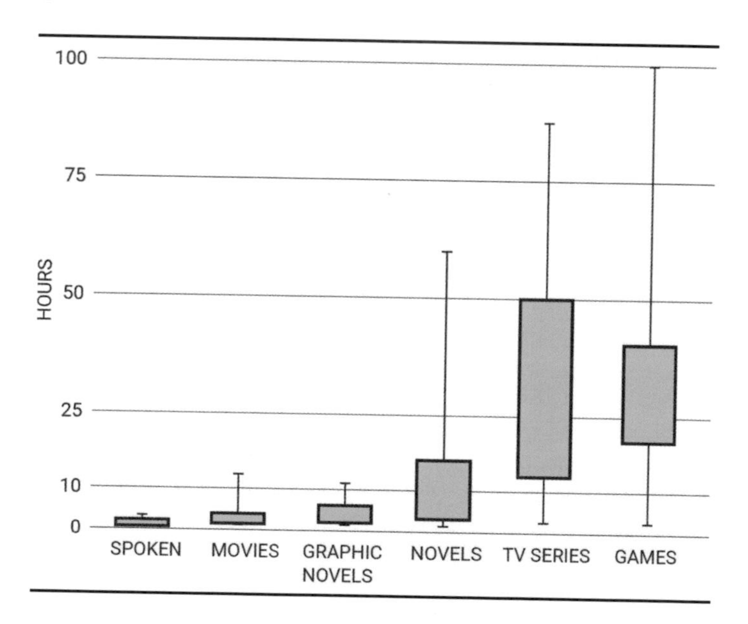

Consumption of media creates reasonable caps on how much information the viewer can be responsible for. Books as a medium must balance exposition with story. Movies have adeptly found the way to shortcut or provide simultaneous information to the audience. This allows 10 hours of content to be compressed into 2 hours. This audio/visual storytelling can provide the audience with nuanced foreshadowing that otherwise would rest in the court of writers. Relying solely on the script to push the story forward limits the imagination and agency of the player to digest information.

Level design must pull from many professions to fully leverage the opportunities available. The visuals alone are an exercise in lighting design, architecture, interior design, landscaping, set design, and urban design in addition to game design. This book will focus on how architecture and interior design can be leveraged more effectively to a narrative capacity. More precisely, we'll look at the way the architecture can have as much responsibility as sound or dialogue to tell stories.

Curating environments to tell a story requires the director to create details which, told through most other mediums, naturally occur. Architecture can provide context for experiences. Whether it's causing delight, excitement, or empathy, humans inherently seek experiences. These can be as minimal as backdrops for photo-ops or as deep reaching as manipulating behaviors.

> *When releasing* Kingdom Hearts 3, *a select few streamers were allowed to play the game in advance to publicize the release. They were asked to play only two hours and to skip cut scenes to avoid giving away the story. Inadvertently admitting to at least two hours of lost opportunity for narrative development and reinforcement of key through gameplay.*

Furniture, light posts, grates, and trash cans all contribute to a functional space but are more opportunities to demonstrate a feeling. From there light posts could appear pragmatic or quirky or romantic as shown in the figure below.

Environments can amplify feelings and prime the occupants for certain events to happen. An environment can convey security or vulnerability.

Materials and craftsmanship can indicate wealth of a neighborhood. Landscape can express sophistication and planning of a cultural or lack thereof. Holding architecture responsible for narrative can broaden a player's imagination as they are ushered into a fictional world.

Patterns emerge as a result of building materials, construction techniques, and site constraints. When the solutions to similar site constraints develop a trend or a style, this is referred to as a vernacular style.

The climate across the United States varies severely and is broken into seven different climate zones. Notably, a building in climate zone 5 or 6 building will have more thermal protection than a building in climate zone 3 or 4. As a result, the buildings in Maine look like "east coast" buildings—they may have brick or stone to retain heat and act as a battery storing a temperature for longer as shown in the first figure below. Buildings in California look like "west coast" buildings which may focus more on cross ventilation and selective use of materials which retain heat. Each has developed a look or style as a result of similar solutions to a consistent challenge as shown in the second figure below.

Learning the possibilities available for any of the patterns can be achieved by trial and error and has been documented over the years in diagrams and details. This learned process benefits almost all contemporary designs.

Physical constraints lock buildings into tropes such that a deviation can develop personality in a rich way, allowing it to reinforce a world as opposed to decorating it or simply providing a boundary. Virtual buildings can take advantage of their lack of physicality, but they don't need to reinvent the wheel entirely. Traditional design constraints can have value as inspiration for virtual design but do not need to be burdened by it.

2

Canon versus Vernacular

Canon and vernacular have been briefly mentioned but may require further introduction. Architecture is about stealing good ideas, continuing a lineage of thoughtful solutions. The buildings stolen from are referred to as "precedents." Canon refers to the academic understanding of architecture worth stealing from. Vernacular refers to a localized understanding of architecture worth stealing from. Yes it is as simple as that. Architecture school curriculums often revolve around the "precedent" method. The reason for this is the "guidelines" architects are often provided for making good buildings. These can come from municipalities, owner groups, even architectural firms. Focusing on key case studies teaches what an architect did with the constraints available instead of what orders to follow.

Academic precedents focus on some core architects that most exemplified the trends. A common grouping is style over time (Zeitgeist), this has fueled revivalist movements or counter movements. Vernacular precedents often emerge in firms looking around to other projects solving a similar problem reliably. If the problem is climate or municipality related, chances are the area will start to develop a regional style.

Whether the proposed design is in support or conflict to the reference building, it builds the design justification. Vernacular on the other hand is ambivalent; the primary goal may be sheltering, marketing, or the whim of the builder or owner. It is identified primarily as "Of local style" or "devoid of an architect." For instance, errors show up in large swaths of brick, you need to drain water every few courses, and may want openings in a wall. It would be wise to introduce some ornamentation, decoration, datums, something to help massage these connections. Alternatively, the design can develop as a reaction to the rhythm of seams forced by construction and material limitations.

A game designer's perspective of architecture differs from the academic approach to teaching architecture. Architecture for entertainment purposes is a fairly recent construct. Game designers may be responsible for rendering a life's work worth of buildings in a 1- to 2-year sprint. They may also find themselves contributing to a chapter of architectural history has been long closed. Much of the built environment is created for and by well-educated and wealthy people. Architectural theory and acknowledgment of construction biases are excellent tools for understanding how existing buildings work. Unfortunately, most critical writing requires some architectural knowledge to comprehend.

Precedent

Lore, legend, critical writing. The lineage of ideas is perpetuated through writing and documentation. Architects are bound to this, whether agreeing or disagreeing with the topic at hand. Moving architecture forward as a profession is a slow task. Writing, realization of work, and dialogue are important to broadening human understanding of space and volumes. It sounds like a lot at first, but really the first step is knowing how to identify relationships.

Canon is the lore of architects and critics. In order for buildings to be comparable, architects and critics create lineages for buildings. This lineage allows buildings to have interactions with each other and create a dialogue. These connections start to allow buildings to define themselves as what they are and what they are not. One could imagine starchitects creating buildings that feed the myths and create new stories. However, not all loud buildings fit into canon, thereby risking falling into obscurity. Much like talking to someone who constantly wants to change the subject, architects are wary about accepting new work into the canon if it is only self-referential or unique to be unique. I suspect that this is the primary reason that architecture is slow to respond to new architecture presented by entertainment fields.

Training in school emphasizes use of built and documented architecture as precedent. Much like legal cases, justification of a design idea can be proven by the existence of a dialogue. From there, critics can use the lineage to critique the idea. Corbusier is a well-known name because he provided manifesto with his work. This framework allows others to join him in creating more architecture in the same family. For example, steel production changed buildings dramatically. Corbusier's five points of modern architecture identify new opportunities afforded by steel. This brought to light a ton of "givens" that were now forced to be recognized as choices. Opening up these new possibilities changed the way that architecture was taught. The technology and documentation in tandem created a paradigm shift which immediately created new styles.

Buildings are categorized and critiqued based on the criteria they appear to be striving toward. Historically variety in design was largely capped by availability of materials and what was successful in the built environment. Modern buildings are sometimes subjected to styles through municipality requirements. Design review processes often set the minimum requirement for an acceptably designed building. In that sense, establishing what you were trying to do allows critics to evaluate the success of your work. That being said, there are plenty of buildings that achieve things they never set out to do, and those that couldn't achieve what they were designed to. Understanding this is advantageous to moving virtual architecture forward. Authentic new work is a result of virtual architecture that does not align perfectly with goals of built structures.

Considering the Discourse

A few tropes have influenced collective consciousness, often the purpose of the building will help sort buildings into genres. Size of rooms are a basic starting point. Modern buildings can subvert this a bit, but for the most part the structural bays will impact the facade. With an open office environment, the core and columns are doing most of the work, such that the layout can change frequently and be customizable for the occupants. Architecture is also subject to a patron system of spending money on behalf of others. This results in architects relying heavily on precedents. These precedents are like legal cases, which indicate what is viable or not viable as a basis of design. The legal ramifications of creating something without a precedent encourage subtle changes as opposed to large changes from existing structures. The perpetuation of this in-turn reinforces the perception of architectural design as a slow-moving design field.

Typologies begin to emerge due to the reliance on precedent works and recurring development strategies. Government buildings often feature glazing and stone cladding elevated on a podium. The windows of the first floor are removed from the grade. This symbolizes stability while literally providing a security measure. Hospitals and hotels work best when rooms are highly repetitive, making experiences fair and equal. This can also save on construction costs and reduce errors in field, which is extremely important for larger and taller projects. When these repeating elements are windows, this begins to codify the façade as well.

Improvement

Architecture is often challenging to critique. Especially when a particularly stubborn designer will not try to interpret why criticism is being raised in addition to the comments they're receiving. Functionally, defense of a design arises from the cause of why it is created. If the building is designed to affect an occupant in a specific way, every detail can contribute to this goal.

The following are Phillip Johnson's list of unrelated defenses to assist in design justification. He lovingly named them the 7 Crutches of Architecture.

1. *History—Because it has worked in another context does not imply that it works without question.*
2. *Pretty Drawings—The design may be beautifully rendered but that does not give credence to the design. It simply serves as a distraction.*
3. *Usefulness—It is expected that the final design must work as is the minimum requirement for a licensed architect. Supposing there is only one correct way to piece together the puzzle when you have created the pieces is simply stubborn.*
4. *Comfort—This originally singled out furniture but can also expand to general audience expectations. Simply creating a comfortable chair is tangential to the goal of creating a well designed chair.*
5. *Budget—All projects have budgets, the architect is responsible for defending their design against value engineering and curating the way cost cutting exercises affect the built project.*
6. *Catering to Client—"Because the client told me to" goes back to the concept of not being able to critically examine and create solutions as a reaction to comments.*
7. *Structure—"Because the structural engineer told me to" also indicates a throw-in-the-towel attitude on the part of the Architect.*

Surely there are parallels in virtual architecture. Defenses that indicate short-sightedness of constraints and ways to excel despite them. Certainly the perfect scenarios setting up a high budget, a like-minded client, and a universal truth to rally the team around are few and far between. Learning how to make a fantastic project despite hurdles is important and valuable as Architecture in particular requires many team members to support a single idea with enough conviction to last 3 years of design and redesign up until the point at which the building gets its certificate of occupancy.

Virtual Architecture—These are not good enough reasons to break immersion

1. *Believability—Virtual Architecture should not find its sole justification in believability*
2. *Spectacle—Any design can be polished and populated with assets and textures, spaces should be critiqued and qualified on their form as well as its polish.*
3. *Familiarity—Choosing a location or strategy should not rest solely on what one would expect the player to already be familiar with.*
4. *Playability—Changes should not be made on the suggestion of play testers alone. Their comments may be indicative of larger problems that they are not privy to.*
5. *Budget—Budget is not a design choice. Acknowledging it is important but should not be an excuse for poor design.*
6. *Catering to the Publisher—Publishers are not required to supply critical feedback, similar to the comment on play testers, they may have found a symptom but they may have the wrong diagnosis.*
7. *Narrative—"Because the story told me to" is not a justification for poor design. Designing something to captivate players need not be capped by the instructions supplied.*

Certainly, design is the culmination of many small decisions made consistently and by a group of people. This is certainly challenging as it is a test of endurance for a team through years of work instead of how passionate any one person is on a given day.

Architecture is rarely devoid of theoretical or physical relationships. Architecture is often categorized by the climates, politics, and time periods, which inflict pressures on the end result. Architectural history is primarily taught by grouping projects of similar styles. Locations and building technology primarily influence "style," from there one could build out a variety of biases at play. Like a table of elements, historians have categorized movements based on narratives and construction methods. At the time architects and artists may not know the way in which they ended up contributing to the discourse. In some cases the nomenclature follows after the natural conclusion of progress toward the style.

Avoiding Derivative Work

Precedents work a bit like a lineage. A work of architecture devoid of this blue blood is slow to be accepted. In part, this could very easily relate to the expectation that nothing is new. Looking to create relationships with existing motifs and patterns and knowing where a new project falls among its predecessors is important to this very old profession. It could also just be architects wanting to show off how many other projects they know. Finding a variety of applications of a similar trait helps distill the way it gets articulated given a new context. Architectural theory is full of endless variations on how environments function or could function. All of this theory is unfortunately available through books with incredibly in depth asides, tangled with references to other projects and colloquialisms. In many cases it's a bit too specific for a casual reader to glean useful material from.

Finding a precedent also means understanding what you want to get back out of it. Say you've found a rendering of an apartment with a brick wall and a metal sliding door. It indicates that the accents are reminiscent of a factory. They look industrial. They're riffing off a collective consciousness created by thousands of interior designers, film makers, and photographers. There are a ton of sources for references of apartments with bricks or find pictures of factories, the goal of course is to not choose based on preference but on adherence to objective. For instance, you could find that metal fans capture your story better, or skylights, or old board floors, etc. This also helps your team and coworkers capitalize on what the direction was from that source. If left only to rely on what grabs attention first, your team can lose focus on the initial vision.

The Antithesis of Canon

Historically, vernacular styles primarily rely on material requirements to determine the ideal form. There's a slightly more recent conversation which actually starts in Las Vegas. The minimum required product to sell services and experiences in Las Vegas, notably, did not follow canon. It was a bunch of massive signs which drew people's attention and brought them into otherwise, un-notable boxes. Robert Venturi and Denise Scott Brown head over to Las Vegas to understand what has been created as a result of market forces. They find that there was an order and organization to success and repetition. Eye-catching architecture was the uniting thread of the new developments. They coined the phrases, "duck" and "decorated shed" to categorize the two ways to achieve this as shown in the figure below.

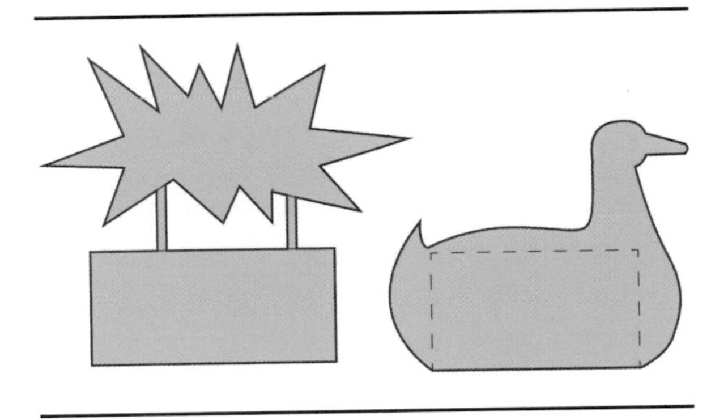

The "duck" allowed itself to forgo a water-shedding, buildable shape in order to become a silhouette. The "shed" was a simple building with a billboard nearby or attached to the facade. These strategies had not previously existed to the critical discourse as an earnest way to create architecture. The problem being that this was someone trying to make a successful building, only they had also created a new metric for success. This identified a new paradigm, a contemporary vernacular if you will. It's the most efficient way to sell products, skimping on finishes, niceties of style and polite nods to previous architects' work. American strip malls most accurately demonstrate the differences in contemporary, not to be confused with modern, design. United States zoning codes are often written defensively to prevent unsafe or short term buildings from becoming the norm. As a result, you're probably quite familiar with the "bare minimum" looking buildings. In almost a complete reversal, virtual spaces are valued on their ability to create feelings and memories as a revenue booster.

Why would canon be important then? Can't everything be discovered through enough A/B testing? Perhaps. Unfortunately, this often curbs toward parodies of spaces as opposed to the invention of a unique and impactful creation. Relying on untrained eyes to curate often results in familiar spaces. Which makes sense—unless you stacked your testing team with multidisciplinary designers and theorists. Interpreting existing structures without requiring another to break them down is crucial to creating new work of the same or better quality.

Architecture is a constantly evolving profession, moving forward on the shoulders of those who came before and passed their learnings down through writing, drawing, and building their thoughts.

Inspiration

A great solution to a design problem can come from anywhere, it doesn't need to be blessed by some architectural deity. From time to time it appears that academic depictions of architecture gloss over the contributions and benefits of work outside of canon. Academically, the most important thing in design is how well you can portray a concept using a compelling space. Professionally, the most important thing in design is not letting your building fall or leak. Naturally great architects are able to marry the two. In order to classify a valid structure ambivalent of canon, critics have dubbed these pieces "vernacular." Historically, it referred primarily to the necessity of shelter as created by local inhabitants of an area. The definition of vernacular as taught changed with is Venturi and Scott-Brown's "*Learning from Las Vegas.*" They identify strip malls and Vegas attractions as a typology. The existing discourse was forced to either provide a rebuttal or accept it. They supposed that there are values and learning moments from the work of nonarchitects in the built environment.

The digital revolution has afforded similarly unique typologies and spatial opportunities exclusively to virtual environments. From a pragmatic standpoint, curating the glossary of architecture to a single timeline and narrative helps students responsible for a smaller breadth of work. On the other hand, work outside of this range has not been indexed and documented to the same extent perhaps as a result. Cataloging design solutions may not have preserved through the years or even addressed yet. Keeping an open eye to the merits of architecture created by nonarchitects is incredibly useful especially moving forward for our industry. Often, these are grouped with "vernacular" styles as the local conditions color the requirements much more than consideration of canon.

The discourse of architecture revolves heavily on precedents, in common language these are just inspiration sources. The dialogue between existing and new work is important for the improvement of a concept. For example, a building or manifesto is a primary source of work, it exists and can be interpreted or portrayed in a variety of ways. The interpretation of a piece by a critic or architect is a secondary source. Abstractions or creation of new work as a result of an interpretation then becomes tertiary. Practicing architects will often rely on primary sources to see what can and cannot be built and if there are failure points, these are not typically the focus of writing and will rarely occur in academic texts. Critics will rely on both, leaning toward secondary;

the context and reaction will have an impact on the meta-community and the legacy of a project. Entertainment industries will often rely on tertiary and primary, skipping over the secondary almost entirely. A lot of the concepts in our canon are straight forward but are unfortunately not easy to learn about. Recognizing the pattern in a vacuum is much easier than recognizing it when it's also conveying other motifs and adopting construction challenges.

Entertainment mediums are particularly underrepresented in architectural writing. This is most likely due to them being relatively young professions, especially game design. The professionals that make up this workforce are often trained in a variety of expertises. Rigor exists within these mediums meriting the addition to architectural discourse. The lack of constraints as they relate to the built environment opens the door to a different variety of spaces. These spaces hold similar constraints to those proposed and proliferated as "paper architecture." This was an exploratory era of architectural studies that supposed surreal circumstances and unbuildable solutions to them.

More overtly creative designs have an opportunity and freedom to incorporate non-building inspiration sources. The language of architecture is still fairly inaccessible. Relying solely on details and motifs heralded as legible by architects may not have the intended narrative impact.

Creating a canvas to have a variety of readings requires some "wordplay." Making something look unsteady can be done by diminishing the support that holds it up. More literal depictions can look like other unsteady things.

> *Studio Ghibli is excellent at this, pulling humble materials into wild arrangements. Specifically, Howl's Moving Castle uses a variety of recognizable sources to draw together the character design of the castle. The castle fuses biological, architectural, vehicular, and mechanical sources to create something completely unfamiliar. The hull of the castle resembles a battleship, articulated with scraps arranged to look like lips of a fish and eyes of a crab. These bellowing shapes embellish its tenuous relationship between its spindly legs and the ground. The exaggeration affords the animation to sway and express dynamism and strain with each breath and with each step. The piles of structures on top are reminiscent of the shell of a hermit crab, accumulating weight as debris grows on it. These support its characterization in a playful but legible way.*

Architectural designs can be a canvas for cultural associations to make impressions. Leveraging the expectation that the audience has some cultural knowledge built up may be more reliable than architectural or historical knowledge. In many cases, entertainment art is incredibly efficient at shortcutting impressions to an intended path. Relying on this to catch the attention of the viewer and give them a piece of the puzzle may also afford them more patience to look for more information in this new canvas. Instead of relying on the viewer to expect information to come from the structure, architecture designed for entertainment often affords a few more breadcrumbs.

Movies are developing a history with architecture in set design, sometimes treating structures to their own character development. Arnheim *Film As Art* acknowledges its merits as a medium worth critique and study. He reviews the works as full of merit regardless of intent or circumstance. Arnheim's hopefulness toward the medium supports the expectation that art is possible through the medium. Though he admits certain elements, such as sound, may have been slow to attract artists in their early stages. Ten years later, Debord's *Society of Spectacle* supposes the societal affectations of embracing "psuedo-worlds."

Games are exceptionally adept at evoking empathy in the audience as they are already interacting and playing as a character. This is fascinating direction for gameplay to move forward because it can make the problems of others seem familiar and relatable. Specifically, creating an emotional impact on an adult audience requires authenticity.

> What Remains of Edith Finch *(2016) depicts the memories of a daydreamer who becomes bored with his life. His daydream overwhelms the playable space, controls, color palette, and music. This change indulges the audience's fascination with his daydream, to the point that it becomes a fixation. "Good" or "bad" isn't necessarily prescribed by the author of this story. It is simply a dichotomy which exists for the player to experience.*

3

Considering the Built Environment

Good design in virtual space is not bound to believability or accuracy. Overcoming this bias can start by understanding how cities and buildings are designed. Everything in the built environment has its own goals and constraints. Knowing more about the reference and how it relates to the active project's goals is important to customizing or abstracting it.

> *Rotoscoping is a great analog to this—animators often use video footage of actors as a reference. This solution came to being because actors and actresses had a more nuanced understanding of body language than artists and provide motion reference for it. Traced actors often fall flat compared to footage that has been abstracted.*

A variety of biases push virtual and built architecture away from each other, construction and physical constraints. Even comparing deliverables can yield an interesting distinction between the two. In some ways both create environments with little to no control over how the content is consumed. The architect must rely on the construction team to create the structure, the artist must rely on the player to control the camera. Even the final build varies between the two, one is a set of instructions to properly construct a building symbolically represented by a 3D model. The other is a literal interpretation called on to evoke feelings as a result of style or side effect of budget. As a result, time and resources are poured into different aspects of the 3D model.

Tools for architectural design and tools for level design are almost completely different. In architectural design, the primary goal is representation of a concept. Game design tools focus on rendering a virtual environment. This primary distinction colors a variety of differences between workflows. A lot of our digital tools focus on building wall as "assemblies" and exporting

2D views of our 3D model with instructions. As a result, renderings are simply a side effect of convincing clients and external team members what intent is. As of 2014 architects are able to preview designs in live render engines without forcing an export to an external program. Our tools still primarily focus on 2D output with the convenience of storing information in 3D.

The tools are also indicative of the biases introduced by industries. Architectural software got really good at making sophisticated boxes before being able to express complex 3D geometries. Divergently, non-uniform rational B-splines, referred to as NURBs, created a way to help architects use more forgiving modeling tools which don't rely on mesh precision and lean instead on parameters or rules. Each software excels at making different designs, it's really easy to push/pull in sketchup, for instance. Offices primarily using sketchup may find solutions that break up the facade by pushing and pulling planes instead of rotating or rounding. Certainly, Unity and Unreal offer these shortcuts, preferring the population of a scene with copies of an object as opposed to subtle variations. As it takes an extra step to get the model out of the editor and into a modeling software, unless the brush was intended to be manipulated, it's hard to justify the premium of changing geometry. Instead rotation, scale, grouping, and color are prioritized.

Architecture is primarily cohesive between the interior and exterior surfaces. Levels, however, are consistently a single plane boundary. This changes the way that spaces unravel. They may become more sprawling, less compact or mindful of the composition. Built structures have "efficiency" percentages to measure how much of the building is usable versus circulation. Reducing hallway area is key as shown below.

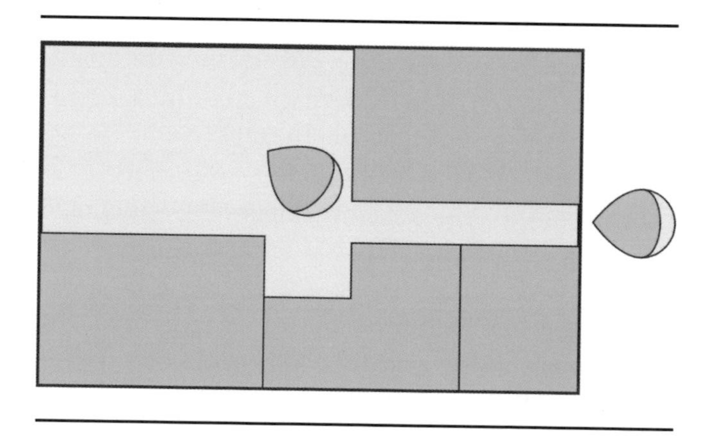

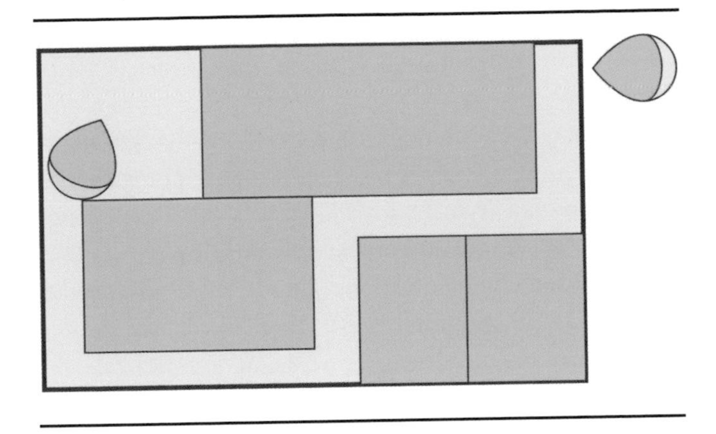

In games, the hallways are often used to provide transitions or build suspense as shown above. It does, however, break the immersion when you're spending most of your indoor time in hallways. Using hallways to peer into upcoming territories can orient players as well as gives them the opportunity to develop strategies as they learn more about the level and enemies. Virtual architecture can rely much more heavily on aging and textures to tell stories about spaces. In fact, landscape architecture and built architecture both heavily design for the optimal moment. Landscape featuring a lush well-groomed illustration of what each plant will become, architecture the opposite indicating the first day of opening for the building.

Virtual architecture has a primary role of telling stories. If the environment is "realistic" it then inherits the constraints of buildings. The success of a virtual environment cannot be judged outside of its intended context. As the goal is not to support weight, repel water, or remain standing for a certain number of years, it cannot compare itself or find merit based on built work. The same is true of built architecture, not able to be judged by pictures or drawings alone. Certain games leverage a cohesive interior and exterior. Ico allows the player to solve puzzles inside and outside of the ruins. The simple decoration and detailing paired with complex and compelling architecture allowed for a thoughtful problem solving game.

Often there's a compelling story available through the way people actually use planned spaces. Occupant usage of a space can characterize occupants themselves and comment on the culture as well. For example, the contrast between densely populated informal spaces and large formal spaces that are empty. The former is charming and can demonstrate a strong sense of community. The latter shows that the community has opted out of coming together when given the opportunity—an adverse effect of the planning of such a space. In virtual spaces this can be posed to correctly demonstrate the intended narrative.

Additionally, virtual environments can capitalize on the opportunity to abstract the literal interpretation of a space. Pixelating or rendering environments with minimal fidelity can provide players with a canvas to imprint their own experiences. In lieu of getting things to be photorealistic, attention to atmosphere, spatial organization, and massing can give the feeling of a space without a ton of additional detail. From there, the design team can use detail to reinforce or subvert the expectation. Borderlands' sobel shader focuses attention on profiles while providing a rusticated and gritty interior texture. *Breath Of The Wild* similarly relies on profiles but has a much friendlier and light hearted approach to rendering. Large blocks of recognizable shapes with a calming color palette. The abstraction and obscuring of visual style has been leveraged in many games.

> Hyper Light Drifter *is incredibly adept at this, large open spaces only seem as such because of the contrast built up over many maps and levels. By creating a sparingly detailed world, they provide enough detail to spark excitement. A non-specific trail off of detail and use of symbols to describe plants and scenes provide a player with ample opportunities to imagine what a literal interpretation of these spaces could become.*

Not only is this a creative way to reduce production costs, it's also a testament to quality over quantity. What is the absolute minimum cue someone would require to get in the intended mindset or comprehend a story. This is something architecture screams but, it is rare to find truly accessible information about architectural theory or intent, it's a bit like screaming into a void. With the help of a story and gameplay, virtual architecture can surpass built spaces in a new and fascinating way of expressing minimalism.

Visual clarity symbolized by groomed paths can find become much more literal. Using height or framing can create much more immersive experiences for players as opposed to the subtle ways things are experienced in day to day life.

> The Witcher III *asked the player to spend a long time playing without intense combat. Breaking up this typical flow, they accompanied the level with a painterly shader to provide visual interest in the wake of this finer grain attention they're asking the player to have. Visualizing this by literally throwing Geralt into a painting may be a bit blunt, but it has the capacity to be compelling in its execution. This is a novel way to bridge the gap of an*

otherwise slow mission by overloading the environment through which the player receives information. Just like looking at a painting in a museum, at a certain point, you get it. The ability to see more affords a longer attention span for searching and finding interest in a work of art.

Many games also must juggle the balance of referenced cities and travel distance. As a result, interpretations of spaces are created by the level design team to allow for the compromise. This disconnect between real and abbreviated invites opportunity to deviate away from the original.

Identifying strategies to take advantage of the medium is best done in the early stages of the game. As previously stated, introducing a new motif in the middle of a project can result in less support through gameplay and narrative. That being said, there is always opportunities to find ways to inherit less baggage from inspiration sources.

Considering Context

The character of a city can say a lot about the history, climate, culture, and leaders that helped shape it. Game environments explore a variety of locations and time periods. The layout of a city is often informed by geography. For a good portion of human history, the success of a city was reliant on access to a body of water. Many large cities begin with a city center is near water. The layout is then informed by time. Technologies, ideals, industries change over time, as a result, cities will have some vestiges of their grown during certain eras. For instance, medieval cities were surrounded by angled walls. Functionally, this was a great defense against foot soldiers and was adopted by cities that could afford to do so. A trait of modern cities is wide gridded roads. The luxury of modern construction techniques make it possible to design the city as a system that is ambivalent of topographical changes.

Cultures haven't always had the luxury of designing cities for the enjoyment of its citizens. Medieval cities had a major responsibility to protect and were typically surrounded by walls. Modern cities benefit more from sprawling than they are inhibited by the lack of safety. Significance and stature are no longer conveyed through fortification but beautification.

A unique set of problems are incurred by cities that keep up with the time. A variety of cultural and social forces necessitate changes over the years. Theories comment on the success of these "collages" and the impact of facilitating new functionality into an existing (in the context of "bricolage"). Changing roads is one of the more permanent and challenging changes. Older areas often result in neighborhoods or communities banding together around what needs to be saved or preserved. In ancient cities, topography and open spaces ruled the design. The expectation for the city to adhere to a single design didn't exist to the same capacity.

Medieval cities start to show a lot of intentionality behind shape and layout of the perimeter. The primary focus on defensibility against infantry is paramount. Walls designed to keep infantry from finding cover. Providing quick passage to positions from the interior and sloped ground to encumber outside attackers, the walls are develop a severe advantage to the defender. Ravelins were incredibly prevalent among medieval city plans as shown below.

This became obsolete with artillery and aerial attacks becoming a primary method of attacking cities. Later, Milan maintained the old city but demolished the wall, as it functionally outgrew this boundary. Ringstrasse strategies propose a ring road where the city wall had once been as shown below.

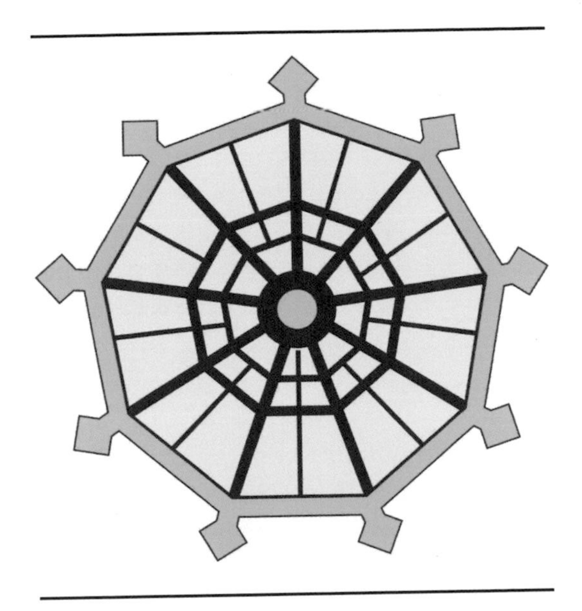

Most modern cities have a planning division that sets up rules for maximum limits for viable buildings. City planners are professionals that work to propose bills to enact city wide changes. That bill is then approved by council members. This allows the city to have some control over the way light and traffic change over time with new development. This affords some capacity to curate a skyline created with a variety of buildings by a variety of architects. Similar to a design document laying out the goals for a level, architects are given zoning information for the owner's parcel. These contribute to livability goals like consistent sidewalks and curbs. They can also create atmospheres and personalities for neighborhoods. Distinctions between street furniture, road width, and green buffer all have a major impact on the pedestrian experience.

By looking at the composition of the city as a whole, relationships can develop at a much larger scale than a single architect could control. Designing urban areas requires a cleverness to description to set the designers up for success and not to stifle creativity while demanding certain qualities. Coordination is required to line up sidewalks and street fixtures is necessary and should be planned at a higher level. Grassroots efforts of individuals creating spaces outside of their lot risk fizzling out or lacking cohesion if not coordinated at a larger scale. Planning also requires the city-level designer to not create unnecessary burden on architects as to avoid turning away potential developers from certain areas of town. These boundaries facilitate a cohesion or common trend through projects much as an art director would request of their team.

Globally, cities develop to suit the needs of their reflective societies. Culturally, it is important to visually depict goals and ideals through the built environment. This also creates a feedback loop for zoning. Zoning is the ruleset that planners use to ensure that they get appropriate buildings for each lot of land. The wording and enforcement of these concepts vary per city and nation. American cities, for instance, are governed by code that protects the city from greed. Japanese cities rely on the society at large to police good behavior. European cities have a tendency to respect historic buildings and lean toward renovation rather than replacement.

It is also important to keep in mind the demographic that is manipulating the built environment. It may not be representative of the ethnic makeup of the city. Progressive cities are able to mitigate the effects of this, the primary challenge is the barriers. It is expensive to become an architect, raising enough money to construct and maintain a building requires funds and experience, and planners must weather political challenges. Additionally, knowing someone in any of these industries is important to success.

> *In the United States, exclusionary zoning and predatory lending have historically pushed minorities out of involvement with development. In tandem, cultural diversity is not always depicted by the built environment despite being a pillar of the cultural identity of the nation. While not related to the intention of modern planners or architects, this historic lack of diversity has inevitably permeated into the zoning codes and building materials.*

Setting up the parameters for a successful city plan requires multiple decades. Ideas must provide flexibility for 5–10 years and have impacts that last 20–50 or more years. These decades of planning result in a skyline. Tall buildings near major infrastructure projects, smaller buildings dissipating out of the city center, slowly fading to midrises and single family areas.

> Fallout 4 *uses Boston as a reference and must find ways to allow it to work with travel times, load times, and interactivity. Identifying locations with opportunities to fill and abbreviate areas is crucial. Boston as an example, is identifiable through key landmarks and what can only be described in lay terms as "charm." More accurately it's a brick walkup and tree lined streets organized to afford cars and sewage safe passage along steep slopes. This is hard to abbreviate, the feeling may be cohesive but the direction and motif are weak. This forces a lot of responsibility onto team members late in the process. In contrast,* Assassin's Creed *finds inspiration through identifiable cities such as Rome, Paris, and Egypt. The landmarks are recognizable and the filler buildings don't have to do a lot of heavy lifting. Rome needs only achieve "classical" looking shapes*

boxes, columns, triangles. Paris only needs avenues and Obelisks. Egypt can rely on massive stone structures. On top of that, they used architectural historians to assist in this process. Also introduced in these games, a mechanism to travel somewhere between running and "fast traveling."

Cities will also hire design professionals or appoint volunteers to critique and evaluate how well a building looks in its context. New urbanists suggest that curating the built environment can foster a healthy neighborhood. The concept of a "street wall" or the canvas that building facades make in relationship to a pedestrian has zoning rules associated with it. Architects are told how tall to make the first floor and how far the facade can set back from the property line. This promotes walkability and prevents development excessively from blocking sunlight. Jane Jacobs' *The Death and Life of Great American Cities* suggests that activity is the means through which safety is achieved. Providing retail and public activities at grade facilitate activity as wells as comfortable depths of sidewalk and integration with parks.

Considering Buildings

Built architecture runs into multiple hard caps on creativity. First of which is zoning, the city has full control over the maximum size of building which can go into a location. The second is the budget, buildings are expensive and architects do not fund the buildings they design. Third is the code and construction, in order to make a safe and usable, buildings are subjected to codes and inspections. Understanding existing buildings may require the consideration of the people who designed them, the people who fund them, and how they are constructed.

Building codes ensure the building will be fire resistant, water resistant, and able to stand despite natural disasters. Accessibility codes ensure the building will be usable by all types of people. Zoning code will ensure that the building will be a good neighbor. The occupancy certificate of the building relies on a signoff of code officials, fire marshals, and inspectors. This creates an inevitability to our constraints. Design is held somewhat accountable by design review boards, but tend to only focus on objective improvements and pre-defined neighborhood goals (i.e., higher quality finishes, designing a certain pedestrian experience).

Funding for built spaces comes from an owner (client). This person or group may or may not have a background in architecture. They are responsible primarily for tracking the budget throughout design. There is usually an agreed upon budget as the project tracks forward, incentivizing lavish designs paired back to moderate ones. This process is called value engineering, the budget is applied to the design, proportioning funds to finish the appropriate portions of the building.

Fire safety also has a major impact on the design of spaces. The primary concern is that the building is able to support itself for 2 hours while occupants exit or are rescued from the building. Providing visible exits and panic-hardware (will not stay latched under pressure) on doors make built structures safer. Often the path of exit out of a building will be clearly labeled.

The anticipation of fire also creates less straight-forward visual impacts, like separating certain spaces.

> *A primary consideration of fire safety in buildings is egress. From a fire safety standpoint stairs and elevators must be enclosed in a 2 hour shaft. Stairwells have footprint repercussions on every floor. The most efficient way to design stairs is to locate them in the same place as they track down. This means moving continuous beams, shafts, and rooms out of the way. Grouping stairs and elevators together into a core reduces the "clear" areas per floor and reduce the overall footprint of the walls required to enclose the openings. For this reason, most buildings have circulation cores. In virtual spaces, these solid walls may not be required. All stairs can be open to the corridor to improve wayfinding.*

For better or for worse, these all create visual impacts on the built structures. This develops a rich texture and character which can be hard to adapt to a new context. Virtual architecture can opt in or out of these constraints as they please. This relationship is much like the freedom animation over film, at the cost of the texture of existing locations.

Architects are licensed professionals responsible for pulling together a lot of different trades and creating a safe building in addition to designing what it looks like. Architects primarily work in plan and section, the whole is just as important as designing the experience on view at a time. Between these two major differences lies, one could see how narrative and concept may at times take a back seat to safety and constructability.

Specifically, the process architects use to develop a design optimizes for agreement and understanding to develop in tandem. Smaller buildings can almost entirely be designed by a single architect. Larger buildings have many more unknowns, the designer becomes reliant on a larger set of relationships with consultants and engineers as well as the client or client group. This gains a further layer of complication when working with city officials and building codes. While the architect is responsible for knowing the letter of the code, the application of the code for an individual building varies per reviewer and a constant improvement of code requirements.

There are five phases to building design—Concept, Schematic, Design Development, Construction Documents, Construction Administration. Each has a different team composition from a management standpoint. Most architectural teams have a hierarchy in place which allows for one designer, a principal in charge, a project manager, a project architect, and design/support staff. At smaller firms, these roles may become merged depending on the skills and desires of the staff, but all responsibilities remain.

- *Concept phase as shown below determines whether or not a pursuit will go through. How many stories can fit on the site, what kind of building does the client need, and do the proportions of the site lend itself to any efficient solutions? All questions that set the premise for the rest of the project. It usually consists of a principal level person, speaking and drawing in shorthand, often with the assistance of production staff to draft concepts. The defense of decisions at this stage is usually based on prior experience, professional opinion, and abstracted precedents.*

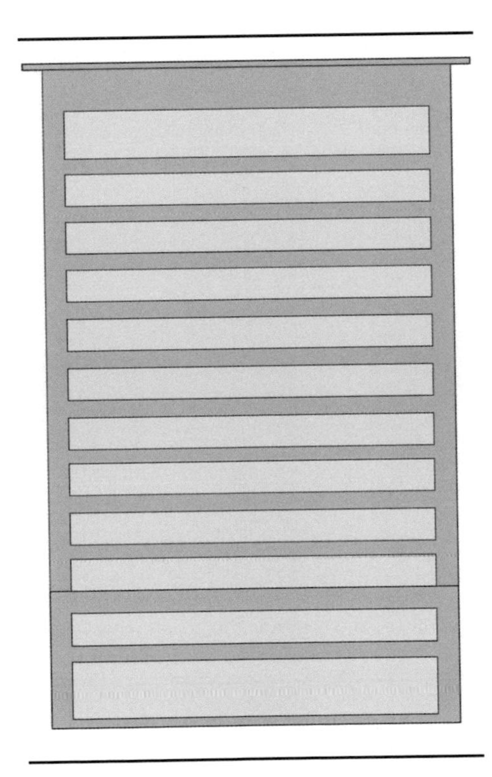

- *Schematic design phase starts to vet the architectural opportunity for the project as shown below. This ensures that the building adequately fits on the site and often will prove that with calculations and diagrams. Engineers and consultants are selected and introduced to the project. Schematic design is a phase that often gets priced for the sake of securing funding. At the very least, a cost per square foot can get estimated based on these drawings. It can also include city-enforced design reviews for public comment. This team will usually merit a principal, project manager, project architect, and 1–2 production staff members.*

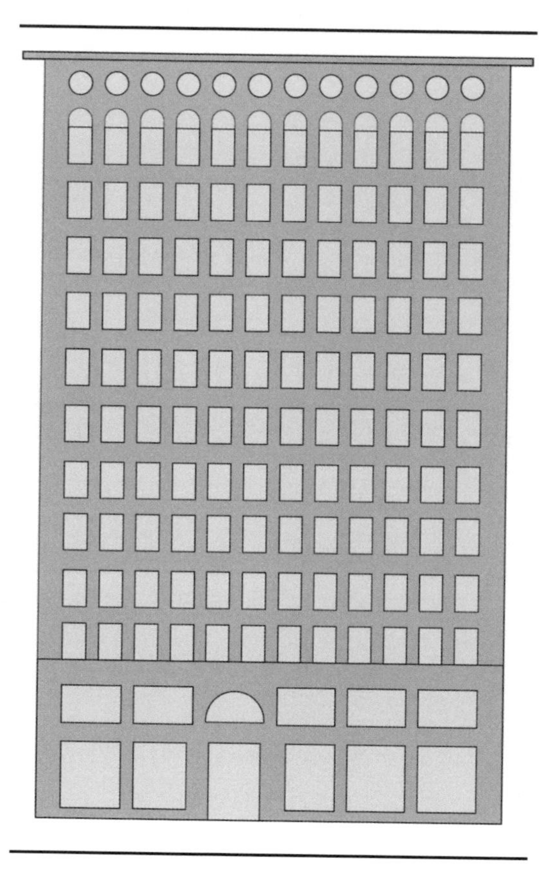

- *Design Development shown below integrates consultants into the workflow and works with a perimeter that is significantly less flexible than before. The walls and floors have specific layers assigned such that consultants can start coordinating more specifically. Another budget checkpoint and city engagement checkpoint can fall at the end of this phase.*

The team adds technical staff members part time. Decisions shift to becoming justified through industry standards more often. The principal-in-charge will start spending less time on the team and get check-ins from time to time.

- *Construction Documentation as shown below is often the final stage of design before breaking ground. The exterior of the building is set for the most part. More details are added to the set, ensuring that individual assemblies will perform their function in the given context. Fire ratings, insulation, acoustics, and weather barriers often rely on continuity. At this point the zoning and building permits are getting completed. This team is its largest and most decisions are justified through industry standards. The large team is able to be directed as a result of this. Often this Principal will be light-touch at this point. Specifications are finalized and agreed to by all parties. Contract documents are created, consisting of a final construction set of drawings and specifications.*

- *Construction Administration is a phase dedicated to the oversight that the design is getting carried out as agreed to in the contract documents (drawings and specifications). All drawings generated additionally are per the request of the contractor, or builder. This may be pre-emptive as they are reviewing drawings or based on new site conditions. Certain trades will not draw their designs and instead build to the site conditions, and as a result, conditions may change from what was originally intended. This group is usually a Project Manager and a Project Architect, pulling in production staff from time to time. Most decisions are based on experience and professional opinion.*

Three things should be evident from this information: The types of decisions made relate to the number of people on the team and there are a lot of "unknowns" that influence architectural designs through the lifecycle of a project. Smaller teams can track more unknowns than larger teams. A lack of consistency is often challenging to larger teams as most changes involve some design choices.

Virtual architecture is designed with tools that primarily focus on design in 3D. Artists are creating their final product as a visualization of a virtual environment. Artists have control to age environments and depict human interaction. This in some ways make the artistic depiction of architecture, in some ways more true than a construction document. Architects will go as far as specifying the type of grout used and the coursing of the bricks, but will not draw imperfections to make it realistic. Architects use symbols to demonstrate intent and provide instructions. Architects spend most of their time in plan and section, using 3D views as proof of concept. 3D views often favor more complex geometries but may influence simpler relationships between parts to the whole. This is due primarily to the fact that architects are providing instructions for another party to create the structure. This lightweight approach to visualization indicates the importance of concept, layout, and articulation to an architectural design.

At the time of writing, we're well into the era of digitally designed architecture. Prior to computer-aided design, doubly curved surfaces rarely existed. Particularly, geometry described through vertices in lieu of equations. This is the equivalent of providing the equation for a hand-drawn line with 100% accuracy. The ability to fabricate with enough precision to ensure connections and assembly on site was granted with 3D modeling. As a result, architects became fascinated with parameter driven architecture. "Parametricism" is a title that implies a bias toward being an end-user. Simply put, requiring the designer to create the tools as well as the project itself creates too much of a bottleneck for talent. Parameter-driven design allows architects to use logical and numerical constraints to design without embarking on programming challenges.

Considering Limits

The built environment differs dramatically from virtual space, primarily because of purpose. Certain design constraints are inescapable. Avoiding practical requirements, i.e., weather proofing often forfeits some control over the finished product. The built structure must have an inspector verify that the building is safe to open, as a result there is an inevitability to getting 100% complete in the built environment. For virtual architecture this reckoning comes if a level is not playable. The repercussions of this can result in a "path of least resistance" approach. Notably, college curriculums will intentionally delay the more practical sides of architecture until the theory and history courses have been completed. While we must abide by them, allowing these constraints to drive our discourse will result in unremarkable and bland architecture. Similar to game design, architecture students are granted a virtual canvas and abstract goals to experiment with. Architectural canon calls attention to a variety of "unrealized" or speculative designs that range from rational to literally impossible to build.

Another source of deviation from pure architectural expression is the source of funding. Generally, there is a notable difference. These buildings were funded by a single family, or sole entity. This fosters a desire for more personality to read through the structure. Contemporary buildings are designed for and, in part, by corporate entities. This results in a bulk of buildings created with the core fundamentals of safe choices and productivity.

Virtual architecture is only bound to the rules agreed upon at the beginning of game development. Some of the major advantages of virtual spaces are scale, material, and occupant mobility. Scale is the first lever to get pulled when something must look more important in many design professions. In virtual applications can leverage geometric limits to a greater capacity than built spaces.

> *A simple example of a threshold not tied to the desired look of a space is the difference between a two-story and three-story opening. From a conceptual standpoint, architects do not prefer two-story atriums. The building code requires extra precautions for three stories without separation in case of a fire event. Smoke evacuation is very costly, as are fire shutters and smoke curtains. If a developer is ambivalent toward the space, they will most likely opt back down to the two story atrium. This diminishes the stock of buildings which have atriums taller than two stories. This actually increases the impact of a three story tall space due to its rarity.*

As geometry doesn't falter over long expanses, the scale of a single plane can be much larger than that of a constructible building. It also of course costs nothing to create a larger space and in some ways can reduce the number of polygons used. Material is a little less obvious as reflections or refractions can slow down frame rendering. For the most part shaders can help pick up the slack, allowing massive marble walls or gold ceilings.

Limitations are incredibly important to acknowledge while developing preferred strategies. Develop a design with the ability to inform. Building materials all have attributes and properties which relate to how they are generally used. Once these traits are identified, it's much easier to tap into the collective consciousness and common associations for these materials.

Another incredibly compelling opportunity for virtual architecture is visualizing the symbolic notions. Corinthian columns are embellished with acanthus leaves as shown below. A stone carving that symbolizes immortality can be virtually depicted as organic. Thriving, defying the bounds of nature to live vibrantly forever. Time also allows for choice, materials can appear worn as it fits the story. Velvet doesn't crush and floors don't scuff unless specifically told to. Designing a city is one thing, designing how it has been destroyed is another. These also are most compelling with the use of a reference.

Designing spaces for nonhuman movement is very rarely considered in other mediums. Architecture must bridge gaps in realism like travel speed and extra mobility given to the playable character. In *Star Wars: The Last Jedi*, BB-8 is perfectly happy on the sand and in a vehicle. As the story progresses, we see him interact with stairs and lose traction, this identifies areas which are beyond his intended reach.

Surprises lead to an engaging and meaningful experience. Allowing surrealism to creep into gameplay mechanics also affords an escape from expectation. Finding opportunities to depart from reality affords designers to use details to reinforce narrative. *Bioshock* lays out levels with sealable glass tubes as hallways, this helps orient the player. They also build in moments to look outside with atriums and large glass windows. This gives level designers some capacity to create a memorable or attention grabbing moment with minimal disruption to the visual palette.

As infinitely many possibilities for spaces are available, priming your player for character and cultural distinctions between locations can be challenging. Maintaining libraries of materials between rooms, neighborhoods, cities, and planets can pay off especially when asking players to retrace their steps. *Nier Automata* uses colors, materials, finishes, and construction techniques to great success as you travel around. This alleviates the responsibility of dialogue or written text to remind the player how rich, poor, war torn, victorious, or intellectual a culture is.

Massing can provide enough contrast to show-not-tell this information. Building this into your design document can help inform the most important content of a concept sketch and can help level designers adapt to late-stage design choices. If stairs would break immersion, finding ways to not just slope floors to get to a point but provide sloping floors intentionally. Look to hiking or skiing for terrain. Levelness of a horizontal surface is extremely important in the built environment, in virtual spaces it is negligible. If you know your character needs more room to move around, consider the ways you would need to actively adapt to change the interior. Understanding typical dimensions of rooms and corridors can inform deviations.

As previously mentioned narrative goals drive design and scope of each building. This allows for a "successful" design solution that doesn't look like built work. Similar to the development of 3D animation, virtual architecture has an interesting job of capturing the familiar and leveraging the new medium to create something fantastic.

> Doom, *for instance, has the layout as a cohesive whole, each level is a labyrinth. The spaces are each designed for multiple engagements as keys may be required to open a door. This horseshoe pattern encourages the player to search walls and find hidden power ups or secrets indicated by small variations in texture. This also provides an opportunity for the player to adopt the character's frantic mindset. This has, while not resembling a buildable structure, served its purpose in the narrative. The game doesn't have to tell you to find secrets or be resourceful as the level design facilitates that gameplay already.*

Architects are constantly reaching for the extents of what architecture can be but of course are constantly running into practical limits of realization.

4

Conceptual Design

Architectural design starts with identifying the scope of exploration. Developing a concept helps focus an infinite world of possibilities to comparable elements. Further complicating this is the fact that game design cannot borrow directly from existing buildings. Success is defined uniquely for built and virtual architecture. Visually, virtual architecture can be "pure" design, not influenced by constructability or gravity. From a narrative standpoint, this gives virtual spaces more potential to be compelling than built spaces. Virtual spaces often have the role of "storyteller" and forgo their role as "shelter." "Authentic" designs are shaped with consideration to means, motive, and opportunity. Establishing where this line is drawn can help teams generate richer spaces without creating an infinite scope. It also provides a rubric for how to create an array of environments. Taking time to prioritize design strategies specific to the narrative can ensure concepts read clearly when implemented.

> Subnautica *uses radiation as a barrier to access the Aurora. The player must create a more resilient dive suit to access the area. Throughout the game, airlocks symbolize safety. The radiation barrier is created by a leakage and not visually revealed. This indicates the type of danger the player will be coming into when exploring the wreckage. A lack of visual cues and reliance on sound clips and data to reveal pertinent information is worked into the quest.*

The primary challenge of creating virtual architecture for the intent of gameplay is that it becomes disingenuous. For instance, you may be designing a hospital but it ends up becoming a stage for combat. Is it a "good" hospital? Are the vertical circulation cores as compact as possible? Is it "good" for directing compelling gameplay? How far does the player need to move between cover? Does the player know where to go next? The functional differences between a built structure and a level can warrant unique design strategies. This puts a bit of a damper on the concept that "believability" improves gameplay. Could the biases that drive gameplay inform of level in a more honest way? The form escapes its responsibility to be a good hospital and more actively work toward the goal of gameplay.

Authenticity is notably the hardest piece of the puzzle to obtain. In order for something to seem believable or authentic it must subscribe to a logic. When developing a concept, these logics present differently at a variety of scales.

Level designers are often asked to create cities or towns from scratch. There are three logics which communities arrange themselves into. One is simply based on resources, villages surround water with little to no need for major planning. The second is a series of plots, maintained by a local government which organically grow over time with a variety of architects contributing (most cities develop like this). Third is a highly planned community, whether focused around a company or a lifestyle, one architect or one aesthetic. The first is simple to fabricate, the second is incredibly hard, and the third is somewhere in between. Mimicking organic growth. Leaning on picture references is the least taxing way to do this. Creating it from scratch takes a lot more thought. As previously mentioned, architecture can be used to portray geopolitical climates and, like clothing, can display wealth. At a smaller scale, architecture can take on traits like characters.

Spaces that relate to existing structures or familiar patterns can evoke experiences from the player. Relying on the collective consciousness, players can be expected to subconsciously pick up on cues. Buildings are often leveraged for their ability to influence people. Churches are designed to inspire respect, schools are designed to encourage optimism and learning. State houses are elevated on stairs to impress a higher level of decorum. Built and virtual architecture can subtly take on this role. Making players feel like they're in control of a situation is challenging, especially when they are learning lore and story.

Developing a sense of place can also have a functional purpose as well. With well-curated architecture and environments, the designer can direct gameplay to naturally flow from space to space. Warming a player up for a platforming puzzle with smaller jumps or priming them with a simple task before asking them to complete a more taxing task. This fields a more immersive environment which may forego tutorials or heads up displays.

Use the environment and lighting to help players naturally perform intended actions. Find ways to integrate storytelling into design and give players more agency.

Defining a Goal

Architectural concepts can have a variety of focuses. Simplifying as much as possible- these have a tendency to start as either 2d or 3d. Planar design strategies can manifest as ornament or texture. Ornamental details contribute to the symbolism in an illustrative way. Textures can provide scale and visualize constraints of construction technology; this is often referred to as Tectonic design. Spatial design strategies rely on forms or composition. These are not poles in the sense that one is the antithesis of the other, and in fact a decision must be made relating to each. Each demands the designer to choose whether it is absent, present, or prominent.

If looking for examples of these design strategies, it is important to note how time has affected them. Ornament was incredibly prevalent through a variety of eras until modernism. Notably, styles like Baroque, Rococo, Italianate, and Art Nouveau champion ornament. Ornamentation typically changes per location and are created by a craft person. Tectonic design relies on the architect using the seams necessitated by materials to create a pattern or field condition. More often, this has been the modernist approach to introducing filigree back into facades and joints. Locating fasteners may be seen by some as a necessary task, but to others can be used to great capacity to further the concept. Some styles that exemplify this would be Brutalism, Chicago School, and International Style. Textures typically create a field condition, relying on repetition and subtle variation to create a pattern. The components are typically standardized and installed per specific instructions. Stand out projects like Adjaye's National Museum of African American History & Culture and Nouvel's Arab World Institute marry ornamentation and texture.

Spatial design strategies shift slightly over time and are primarily triggered by major shifts in technology. Figural designs focus on forms and profile. Certain styles like Mannerist, Futurist, and Post-modern use this to convey abstract concepts. Improvement of CAD software increased the ease at which architects could achieve this design goal. Concepts that use composition to justify locations of architectural elements often rely on logics outside of the specific project. The outside logic may be canon or a manifesto, justifying the series of works academically. These compositionally driven works can work visually for a lay-audience but the rationale may not be easily reverse engineered. Every once in a while, an architect will equally prioritize these two together. Frank Gehry and Zaha Hadid both had good academic understandings of composition before leveraging digital tools to apply these rules to less traditional forms.

The ability to suspend disbelief is the most important contribution levels can provide to your player. Leveraging this requires the designers to tap into as well as author new content to a collective consciousness. It also requires the designer to trust the player to fill out the story in a way that's personally meaningful. This is a fine line to walk, triggering things that are meaningful to them, guiding them to actively apply them to your story. In movies, this is done by pairing an emotional moment with a variety of related incidents. People can relate to emotions like love, disgust, anger, righteousness and will sympathize with characters and situations. Appealing to a player's individual experiences allows them to record the memory as a participant in the story rather than an observer.

Players are incredibly adept at using their personal experiences to color the way they perceive your game. Intentionally giving enough of a breadcrumb to give them a canvas to project a meaningful experience on or sparking creativity in the player by giving them inspiration are the ideal poles of this spectrum. Too far in either direction could leave them confused with a lack of information or over explaining to an audience that may or may not perfectly match the anticipated comprehension level. Relying too heavily on collective consciousness allows your designs to blend with familiar elements. Identifying a unique characteristic to tie to the game consistently can reduce the temptation of bland solutions.

> Doom *relies on pixelated renderings of flesh or grotesques on walls to depict an idea of what would be there. While this is a side effect of graphic limitations, it had a meaningful impact.* Quake *and the reboot of* Doom *were able to render these with more accuracy but varying levels of success. The fearlessness of achieving something that wasn't easily rendered was carried by the players. Players were able to see that this was different than other environments, mimicked terrifying enemies, were able to imagine something much scarier than what was illustrated with real time graphics.*

Architecturally, designs can play into this by subscribing to popular solutions to recurring design problems. Biases in architectural design often begins in the form of "Path of Least Resistance." Understanding the origin of these biases is helpful to making more informed decisions while still pulling inspiration from great works. Most importantly, they can prevent you from inheriting tropes which may not apply in their new context. We'll sort out common design solutions ranging from urban planning to joints in materials.

A few tropes have influenced collective consciousness, often the purpose of the building will help sort buildings into genres. Size of rooms are a basic starting point. Modern buildings can subvert this a bit, but for the most part the structural bays will impact the facade. With an open office environment, the core and columns are doing most of the work, such that the layout can change frequently and be customizable for the occupants. Architecture is also subject to a patron system of spending money on behalf of others. This results in architects relying heavily on precedents. These precedents are like legal cases, which indicate what is viable or not viable as a basis of design. The safety of deviating from the built environment in subtle ways visually contributes to what is expected of architecture.

> *Government buildings use this material, elevated on a podium. The windows of the first floor are removed from the grade. These buildings don't necessarily need a ton of daylight, especially at the expense of a security vulnerability. Hospitals like to give rooms windows in the same area, so we see a lot of repetitive conditions which cover large swathes of facades. High rises tend to focus on a similar strategy, achieving it through a variety of systems based on cost.*

Other design fields leverage psychology and expected responses are graphic design and user experience. Relying on learned and previously applied actions can contribute to readability and usability.

Having a Parti

One of the most important contributors to a successful concept is clarity. A parti is a diagram of the concept. Distilling the concept to a diagram affords interpretation with direction. Developing a system helps deliver the concept to players. It also allows others to contribute to a concept while still having creative freedom. Some room for customization throughout the design process leads to a more resilient product, adapting to changes. Sequencing spaces or levels as a series of diagrams can help to clarify the relationship between them.

Clarity in concept also allows for deviation as you learn more through research and creation. More often than not, ideas won't work out exactly as planned. Architects accommodate mechanical equipment or structural loads. This shouldn't cost a full redesign for the project every time something changes. Working with a concept that allows for multiple correct answers affords flexibility to the team. Levels must still ultimately accommodate and support gameplay. Interesting design that doesn't help gameplay can complicate teamwork and distract from immersion.

Some of the most replicated gameplay experiences started as a really well executed solution to a problem. Games have a unique set of constraints and opportunities not present in any one of its neighboring mediums. For instance, UX design for games can be much louder than something outside of a game environment. There's an absolute ton of information game designers can use to get started with a new UX/UI strategy hinged on years of graphic design theory. Informing decisions with context specific adjustments can create more intuitive and fluid acclimation to the environment.

Super-human movement is very rarely considered in other mediums. Architecture must bridge gaps in realism like travel speed and extra mobility given to the playable character. In order for the fictional world to have weight, the architecture must abide by the physics and socioeconomic constraints laid out through the storyline.

Architecture is about improving with each iteration of a concept, successors call these inspirations "precedent." This harkens back to the use of them is justification as well—positioning it as a piece of evidence. Leveraging others' work as design justification takes a bit of reverse engineering. That's where knowing a bit about construction, biases, and history can reveal intention. The consequence of this is a more nuanced variation between built structures. This facilitates new opportunities for meaningful experiences for players. Authenticity requires understanding of opportunities and knowing constraints well enough to create remarkable results because of or despite of them.

A major benefit of looking to architecture to find inspiration and direction is the variety of interpretations and memories it can evoke. Light can be controlled to diffuse or beam, pulling from predictable channels. Diffused light will come from a north facing window, this is a reserved and calm way to invite light into a space. It can also be directed in with light cannons, acting as spotlights and painted to act like a gel. Goals of architecture can be nuanced and at times more complex than a sketch or diagram can lock down. From a more practical standpoint, seeing a built structure provides information about constructability and provides opportunities to push a concept further

Examining the precedents more intensely can help inform why details were used. There's a whole lore behind what leaves, fruits, and ribbons are carved into column capitals. It can provide a trajectory for future projects or reorient toward a more accurate representation of what is important in a concept. Learning from and adapting to new information is a major distinction between successful and failed buildings. Adapting to a new understanding of a concept is a major benefit of using architecture to tell stories, like narrative, it can hold multiple readings as the player sees more levels.

> Ori and the Blind Forest *leads the player through the story by having them develop skills. By unlocking them over time, the player can to get into new areas, previously unnavigable. This allows the reuse of geometry in a clever way as the change in gameplay changes the experience. A previously risky jump is now easy to span with a double jump or grappling hook. This variety helps the player focus on different, previously overlooked details. It doesn't feel like repetition for the sake of stretching a game out.*

In turn, the more times an idea is used, stolen, or reappropriated, the more nuance it develops in each application. In most cases, a good amount of narrative design relies on an overlap of previously consumed media. This is often leveraged in visual media to great avail, perpetuating an understanding that simplifies the narrative. Tropes are incredibly useful for making an impact quickly.

The framework which affords the user to freely interpret their environment must be carefully curated. Building a system to design within is challenging. Rules which help provide continuity for concepts can also create predictability inadvertently. Rules prevent architects from accidentally creating a harmful structure. Our rules come into play over hundreds of years of failures and sharing information. Some no longer apply but have become so entrenched in the look and feel of a structure that they've remained as "rules" nonetheless. This build up over time creates a lot of quirks and interesting moments as a result.

> *Compare the* Fallout *series to the* Bioshock *series, noting the way a post apocalyptic worlds describe an even that freezes cultural development around 1950. This forces either culture to coast on the artwork and architecture of the time. (Suspending disbelief of how practical it is to expect this in either scenario.) We see a necessity to provide nuance to prevent the games from otherwise running together.* Fallout's *world relies on new architecture being created has a hopeful look with new buildings kludged together. Bioshock's world relies on a more nuanced understanding of the age of the*

unchanged building as the inhabitants change. From there you may develop pockets that embraced futurism, streamline modern, or internationalism. Alternatively, you would find brutalist works, bunkers, humble structures.

Finding new ways to use multiple patterns together without conflicting or becoming noise unintentionally. In short, the information will ramp up pretty quickly as we get into construction of theoretical concepts. When hammer meets nail, the familiar symbols we use to represent designs become textured and heavy. Alternatively, that clarity of intent is best indicated by the symbols; the marriage of the two is essential to understanding the scope of influencing factors. Due to the fact that physical constraints are not introduced in virtual environments, supposing the constraints becomes part of the worldbuilding exercise. A lot of texture which is generated out of necessity must either be introduced as ornament or eliminated. This decision is not without repercussions, as many designers have noticed. Clever and imaginative mechanical solutions have been introduced to make buildings look more industrial. For some reason this is something which people feel quite comfortable authoring.

These distinctions color the experience your player has. Helping them fill in gaps and generate new ideas and in turn create new stories as a result of the setting you've provided them. The framework inspires great solutions. Bernard Tschumi famously notes "[Architecture] cannot satisfy your wildest fantasies, but it may exceed the limits set by them." The capacity to make a game unforgettable with the help of architecture appears to be unbounded by genre.

Doom II *actually uses both distinct place making and abstract textures baked into the game environment to provide lore and strategic information to the player. It trains the player over a series of levels to navigate the halls of hell more adeptly.*

Following Through

Cohesive design can lay the foundation for immersive storytelling. A key feature of achieving suspension of disbelief is consistency. This allows the player to err on the side of using their imagination to work toward immersion. Convincing the player to enjoy a moment or arc isn't always straight forward and requires attention to detail. A challenge with the games as a storytelling medium is the duration of the story. Going from what a typical movie would be (3 hours) to something around 100–300 hours of content, there are some challenges. First, your game may not be played in a single sitting. This in and of itself creates a multitude of immersion challenges. Second, it may not be episodic or designed in digestible chunks. Game designers can rely on more subtle communication methods through form and environment design to avoid repetitive lines of dialogue. Architectural design can communicate "constant beats" to players. Like a mind palace, the player has the ability to tie the beats of the story to spaces if they have meaningful correlations. 3D Environments can also expand on the implications of a worldbuilding choice.

As a result of nuclear fallout, all spaces are either hermetically sealed or indoor/outdoor. This differentiates the prepared versus unprepared, it demonstrates a spectrum of radiation exposure as a result of the impact.

Games which rely solely on dialog to re-enforce plot or character beats run the risk of sounding redundant over the course of the whole game. The level can be used as a consistent and subconscious vehicle for storytelling elements.

> *Movies lean heavily on architecture for a reference point for sets and tone. The Bradbury building in SF is a well known location for shoots but has taken on many different characters. By using understanding the source material and leveraging different sides of the building's character, directors have pushed the building to play different roles in the plot.* 500 Days of Summer *uses it to inspire hope and impress an idea of rigor,* Blade Runner *uses it as a vestige of the past and serving as a jumping off point for the future as portrayed in the movie. Both use the building to indicate trajectory by finding nuances and fascinations in its details and layout.*

Consistently telling one story and using every means available to bolster the concept does require some curation. Knowing when to stop telling and start showing will also depend on who the target demographic may be and how crucial that information may be to the story. Asking someone to learn an entire world upfront may be overwhelming and alienate people outside of the comprehension level that the copy is written for. Relying on the environment for indirect exposition facilitates a flood of information available for player to digest as they choose. Learning a bit about architecture can help demonstrate to players may leverage their own experiences more acutely. Leveraging someone's personal memories is a better way to create an intriguing experience for them. Triggering this is way easier to do with the help of visuals. Identifying how challenging it is to create props for movies and maintain historical accuracy is much easier in virtual spaces. Old cars, fashions, buildings, can all be conjured up by artists based on photos. As a result, using virtual spaces to reimagine historic environments led to the advancement of new technology.

> Bioshock *authored unique content to streamline modern and art deco chapters of design. They not only reproduced existing art deco themes, but also created new streamline modern masses with art deco ornamentation.*

Architects often have objectives for occupants, as a result, virtual games should have a similar standard. For instance, designers often leverage signage or wall orientation to grab the occupant's attention and direct them to another space. From there, the environment can use textures to codify the circulation passages vs destinations. Further still, lighting fixtures can make the occupant feel welcome if upgraded from standard fixtures. Using the budget to create comparative relationships between spaces allow more precise control over the experience a person has. Things like ceiling tiles or linoleum floors make a space feel cheap because of the environments they're typically paired with. Environmental cues can relay information in a variety of ways. They can range from attention grabbing to influencing occupants below the level of consciousness.

People are incredibly adept at reacting to spaces, even if unable to verbalize what caused the feeling. In order The feeling of cohesion is often achieved below the level of consciousness. Architecture is actually fantastic at this as it requires no acknowledgment to have an impact.

Architecture has the capacity to affect occupants, whether it's behaviorally, portraying a sense of place, or providing a lens to perceive information. Creating an environment which allows for interactions to become personally impactful. "Place and Occasion" are ascribed by the occupant.

Levels work in similar ways, organically teaching strategy, providing a backdrop for lore, and divulging plot. Integrating and making meaningful all portions of the level and even UI elements. Building this expectation with the player contributes in a small way to the overall immersion. Rewarding curious players with information for their thoughtfulness primes the player to find more information in their environment.

Part II

Massing

So far, this book has indicated the theoretical groundwork of architecture. The application of that first materializes in "form." Providing this step allows for critique with limited distraction. As architects develop massing studies, they look to build relationships between spaces. They look to build relationships between spaces. They also look to identify pinch points and scout out challenge areas.

The way architectural elements are strung together can imply to an audience a more complicated story. Form is where that story starts for the design team. Starting with a concept that scales and forms which provides multiple "correct" answers will help reduce redesign later. In architectural practices this allows decisions to come at a time where they are less expensive to implement.

> *As time progresses, massing changes trigger larger ripple effects with the project. Moving the elevator core after the structural engineer has designed the foundations under each column costs engineering time in addition to drafting time.*

Setting up designers for success is a primary goal for early stages of design. The concept must be resilient enough to still maintain its integrity after learning more about the constraints of the project as shown in the figure on the next page.

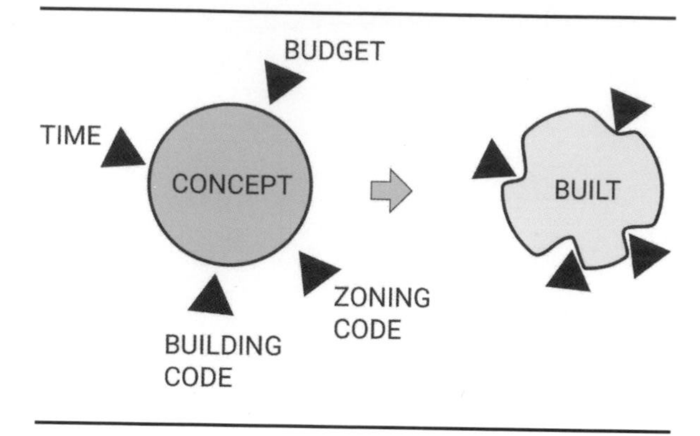

Providing some room for designers to be creative and still adhere to the original concept is important.

> *Architects identify the least malleable components of a building and define them first as shown below. This is typically the exterior and exiting as the building footprint affects many different trades and life safety is a primary requirement. We sketch and model to come up with interlocking organizations of spaces. From there we see what constraints introduce themselves. Large changes run the risk of nullifying previously resolved problems.*

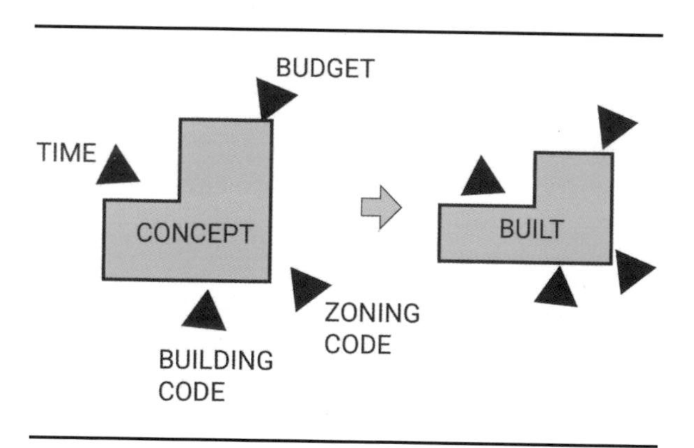

An architect will start with simple understandings and diagnosing challenges with the site, context, and constraints of the geometry. This maps pretty well to the considerations and experience.

There's a massive benefit to getting things right the first time, especially when mechanical, electrical, and structural engineers are basing everything off of the architect's geometry. This puts a huge emphasis on a successful schematic design—or grey boxing. This can be achieved by having a vision which doesn't rely solely on a single moment or gimmick. It also requires the initial designer to have a very good idea of what constraints generally reign over the typology. For instance, garages have a different column spacing than the floors above, dodging the drive aisle when locating the elevator core is extremely important, even if it isn't glamorous.

Architectural design is broken into phases, concept, schematic, design development, and construction documentation. This tracks fairly well to the way architecture is taught. Most undergraduate programs focus on concept design. The first few years are focused on history as a reference and abstract design thinking. This prevents information overload and focuses critique and justification on concept and schematic design. The curriculum leverages the inexperience of the candidate to build desires that aren't anchored by biases or constraints. Supporting classes give information on theory, construction, physics, structural design. By the end of undergraduate studies, an architect-in-training could expect to design a competent building to the schematic design level. A decision point comes to continue with academia or pursue an apprenticeship. Whether in graduate school or as an apprentice, one could expect to learn about building systems from related consultants.

Identifying concept goals and setting up the environment to frame them can help reduce rework later. Big changes get harder to make as development moves on in a project. Resolving composition early yields the widest variety of solutions. Especially when working with a team, grey boxing can be used to shot-call or direct a team to a successful composition with minimal coordination effort. Making spaces that seem familiar in proportion and scale can help enforce similarities or provide a "control" variable from which to derive differences.

> Subnautica *sets up soft boundaries that relate to safety. The designers use plants and creatures to smooth the transition between biomes. Players mimic different scales of fish as demonstrated through gameplay. Small edible creatures stick to the shallows. This has plenty of starter material. As the story gets divulged, the player gains the ability to become more resilient. Players begin to mimic larger fish and can traverse larger or deeper biomes. The largest areas are populated with leviathan class creatures that can sneak up and destroy the player. This becomes relevant when caves come into play, going from a constricted safe space to a massive cavern, signalling a danger again.*

To some extent, as a designer, you must reward the player for pouring their own thoughts into the experience. If you set a standard that ceilings are rewarding and worth looking at, you'll train your player to use that information actively. If you mail it in, you're likely to lose a bit of that trust with the player. It's kind of like sig-figs. How do architects build these expectations? We'll go through a quick study noting specific elements and their impacts. Architecture can be described through its materiality, adjacency, figure, light, and scale. More complex ideas such as proportion and ratio can be extrapolated from "scale" for instance.

> *Zaha Hadid uses the Contemporary Arts Center in Cincinnati to make art accessible. She uses a variety of tactics to achieve that accessibility, tackling it from different directions. Hadid ushers the public in by continuing the concrete from the sidewalk into the building and up the wall. This gesture also allows the concrete to characterize itself through texture. It's scored and rough at the sidewalk, honed in the lobby, and has a formwork texture as it turns into a wall. The massing of the building relies on sliding gallery "boxes" indicating function. She shows how the exhibition spaces are laid out via the facade. Direct sunlight isn't good for art, therefore that space will be devoid of functionable windows. This also indicates individual collections and creates a hierarchy for understanding their relationship. Natural light, indicating public space, is completely glazed—not punched openings. The vertical scale of the public spaces also allow for the natural light to reach deep into the structure. The exaggerated lighting contrasts public space from exhibit areas which cannot be naturally lit. This provides an intuitive cue for the occupant to speak quietly or move slowly in gallery spaces, while still providing a visual relationship to the vertical circulation. So there's a lot of moving pieces in this one—all working to make art seem accessible. Hadid pursues motive from a variety of angles using multiple design tools. This adds to the impact and legibility but also an opportunity for improvement for architects using it as inspiration.*

Let's take a moment to suppose the sentence structure of architectural design. We have at our disposal materiality, figure, scale, proximity, and phenomenology. Somehow our goals can be visualized using these tools, whether leveraging existing biases or creating new patterns. Recontextualizing existing motifs or trends will change them and is a valuable exercise. Creating an existing building in a virtual environment traversed by a character in a fictional world will yield a unique experience, even if geometrically similar. One challenge is that some of the most expertly designed buildings have motives for their occupants, if copied with no attention to its original intent, it may send mixed messages. Using existing architecture and game environments, we will break down what spaces say using figure, scale, and proximity.

5

Function

Given current building materials and typologies, form is often informed by function. One of the primary reasons is quite boring—money is being represented by client groups. Day-to-day decisions are often made by a representative of the client. The ability for the architect to do something "just because" is incredibly rare, as that representative must justify a potentially risky or expensive decision to investors or financiers on behalf of the architect. The other reason lies within materials. Modern architects sparingly employ ornamentation as a design tool. The lack of ornamentation grows with the proliferation of manufactured materials. Manufactured materials get cheaper and more durable every year. Paying a premium to introduce a layer of ornamentation for the purpose of disguising breaks in material is no longer necessary. As a result, form for form's sake is not often available as a design choice.

Finding the cross section between what a space needs to do and how it should look often comes through understanding the problems at hand. Biases introduced by the way a space is being used can bring forward unique design solutions. Design concepts and project management can both benefit from considering this at a high level. Architects use diagrams to identify patterns and relationships between forms before diving into any precise solutions. Understanding the path of least resistance is an important step to solving any design problems. This provides a control variable for design iterations as well as a reasonable stopping point if the immediate team cannot accommodate the task in sequence.

A common goal for architects is to reduce the footprint of the building. This is the simplest way to reduce cost through geometry by reducing surface area. Developing an optimized solution allows the architect to make precise decisions about where to deviate from this or define the requirements for the quality of a space. This exercise may be different for a level designer. You may need to design for an interaction to happen every 5–10 seconds in a city and every 2–5 minutes in an open area. Spacing out interactions can help inform massing or design as a means of developing cities that aren't just compact versions of built environments.

This tetris-like planning affects the look and feel built structures. Buildings with rentable space in them are typically more efficient. Buildings with a long-term tenant, which won't change hands often will have a more relaxed outlook on how far they'll go to reduce circulation area. In fact, many museums celebrate and leverage it to emphasize an exhibit or create a dramatic procession. Game design leverages this tactic often as the story or gameplay may benefit from a corridor to restrict opportunities for flight, forcing a decision point. This does, however, seem foreign as most places with elongated hallways celebrate them by allowing them to be open to nearby spaces.

Humans navigate virtual and built environments differently. A primary example would be the effect the sun has on the player. Often, open spaces are used in the built environment based on how well they can provide shelter from the elements. In warm climates, protection from the sun is incredibly important to parks and open spaces. People will sit under trees for shade or by water to stay cool. Providing shade would not attract a player controlled character in the same way. Moves in the built environment can be justified by the way a human feels. A pedestrian may choose a path with more shade or a shallower slope. If it's raining, more overhead cover, shorter trips outside. These are all reactions to feelings that often require additional mechanics when in virtual environments. Bars simulating heat or rain obscuring views can direct players in similar ways, ducking into buildings. Moves made in virtual space are typically either strategic or self-preserving. Players can identify strategic moves through sight lines. Players can identify self-preserving moves by imagining what would provide refuge and where that could be found.

Game design is similar to set design in the sense that, if the story doesn't require a room to exist, no one would have the ability to check if your building was cohesive or if a second-story room would significantly overhang the first floor. Meanwhile, there are opportunities to provide this relationship for the player, as a means of orientation or exposition. Preparing for a dramatic moment can be foreshadowed with a glance into a grander space.

Half-Life 2 and *Bioshock* both leverage this spectacularly. As a player, you understand "public" and "private" areas as they relate to each other.

This primes your player to want to use stealthier gameplay without having to be told. In *Half-Life 2,* spaces like homes and sewers feel safe. Single-story spaces with limited ability to be seen or sniped feels good to spend time in and aim out from. Adversely, large open areas make the player feel vulnerable. Public buildings or tall ceilings leave a lot of opportunities for surprise. Smaller spaces are knowable.

Bioshock also found an appropriate vehicle for giving players this agency. Using windows into unfamiliar spaces, levels were able to spark curiosity and push the player to explore. Catwalks, windows, and cut scenes selectively remove temptation, and ultimately agency, to intervene. This dichotomy is then leveraged to unite the player's and the character's perception of events. Ultimately, having spaces that are adjacent but not accessible takes some curation. Using arcades, atriums, and lobbies, levels like the medical pavilion and fort frolic get a ton of mileage out of central spaces. These areas provide a sense of familiarity and can be laced with foreshadowing elements as the player moves through them multiple times. Unlocking different abilities within a level allows the player to develop different strategies and adds replayability.

Identifying Opportunities

There are infinitely many types of games out there. Similarly, building typologies can vary wildly between function, context, and culture. It's important to identify givens or biases introduced by the type and use design strategies that acknowledge them. This is also true for building materials.

Taking the time to study what types of moments often happen as a result of game typology can inspire more clever design solutions. For instance, if you're designing a side scrolling game, what makes gameplay exciting? Using diagrams to identify this for a set of levels or a game can help teams reach decisions and provide a rubric. If it's movement about the screen, the diagram finding ways to branch a linear movement or break datums. If it's about using certain mechanics, breaking down what keeps players in motion and what would stop them would be a great way to have functional control over the pacing.

Identifying patterns and leveraging them as a basis of design provides a great starting point for a logical structure. Subverting this or creating a wilder solution can then become a comparison. The team can take a more organized approach to the challenges created by developing a more stylized solution. This facilitates a measured approach to a knowable problem which often looks far more graceful than something introduced as a "fix" at the last minute.

Identifying Constraints

A great place to start designing is by spatially organizing the minimum viable product. Architects use placeholder forms to ensure that our solution is tailored to our program and constraints. Organizing this information as it fills the site allows for specific solutions and patterns to emerge. Massing or grey boxing allows us to prioritize spaces and control which spaces flex. Inevitably, designers can only anticipate so many constraints before developing the scheme further. While the specific challenge of envelope or the extents of the building may be subverted in virtual space, boundaries and constraints still exist. Blocking out the playable area, using that to determine vision extents is important for scoping your project. It is important to intentionally select which details gain more specificity as it relates to time spent in a space. Identifying level of detail and planning accordingly concept can prevent rework and scope creep. A good designer can set up all support staff to create work that fits with initial vision. Solving all problems personally is not always an option. It's also not bad to do this for yourself. It is easy for designers to find inspiration and change directions within the course of one project. Putting in extra work in the early stages to reduce unique scenarios and geometries is helpful down the road.

The best way to ensure that our pieces accommodate each other is by using modules and grids. Gridlines help give spaces definition and character before forcing massing decisions. These are used in built structures for coordination with the structural engineer and contractor. It also helps ensure that walls stack correctly and spaces stay efficient as they stack. The architect and structural engineer will locate grids together and adjust by inches as the project moves forward. Gridlines also work as a design organization tool, defining datums and preserving relationships.

The grid helps locate spaces in a way that continues to organize as long as rules are followed. There's not a ton of deliberation of the precise location of walls, the grid line becomes the datum as shown below.

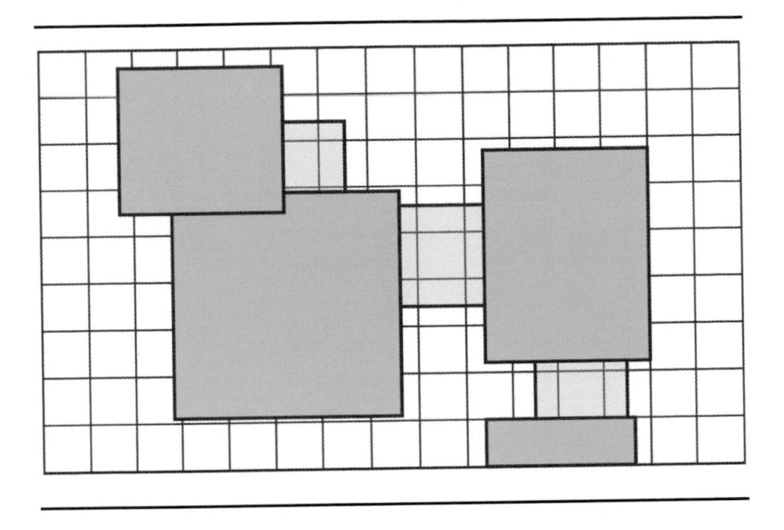

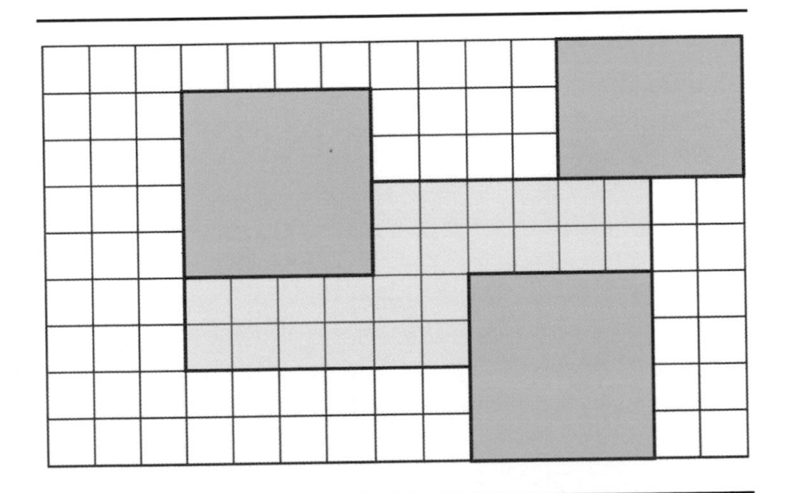

Corridors can start to follow similar sets of rules. Describing the point of connection for adjacent rooms also becomes important with more team members. This also helps plan for spaces and breaking off pieces for collaboration. This also allows nimble transitions between options before committing it to any certain orientation.

In built architecture, the interior fills the envelope. In virtual architecture, the two need not intertwine perfectly, or even at all. From there the freedom introduces interesting biases. I'll show you a typical layout for a house versus a level taking place in a house. Understanding the route of travel vs

FIGURE 5.1
Compact Envelope Circulation Study

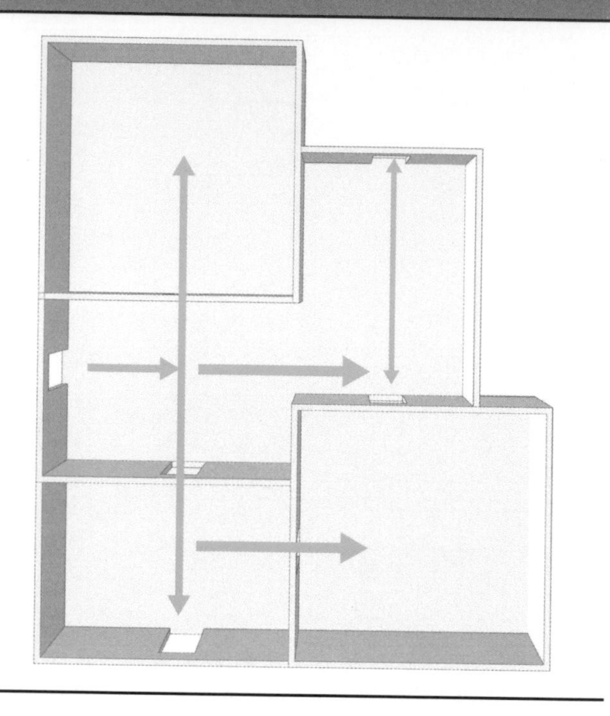

functionality of scenes will open an opportunity to create a cohesive space. In our profession this allows for a more compact footprint, which typically is not a high priority for game designers. The side-effect of this is that multiple spaces can work in tandem, sharing only a visual or atmospheric connection (phenomenal transparency).

While prefab puzzle pieces may be easy to chain together, it is very easy to wind up with a "hallway" type of level. This can lead to disoriented players and missed opportunities to build spatial emphasis without scaling up. Player scale is no new concept to level designers, a general understanding of scale is required to create successful and challenging platforming.

There are some major benefits to a more consolidated footprint when organizing rooms. Compare the compact envelope and linear progression circulation studies as shown in Figures 5.1 and 5.2, respectively.

Primarily, buildings benefit from small perimeters and reduced circulation area. Virtual environments leverage hallways to pace or stretch a story out. Hallways can build suspense, give the player time to consider an environment and control the route players take through a level. This ultimately affects the player's ability to compare spaces and limits it to a sequential understanding.

FIGURE 5.2
Linear Progressions Circulation Study

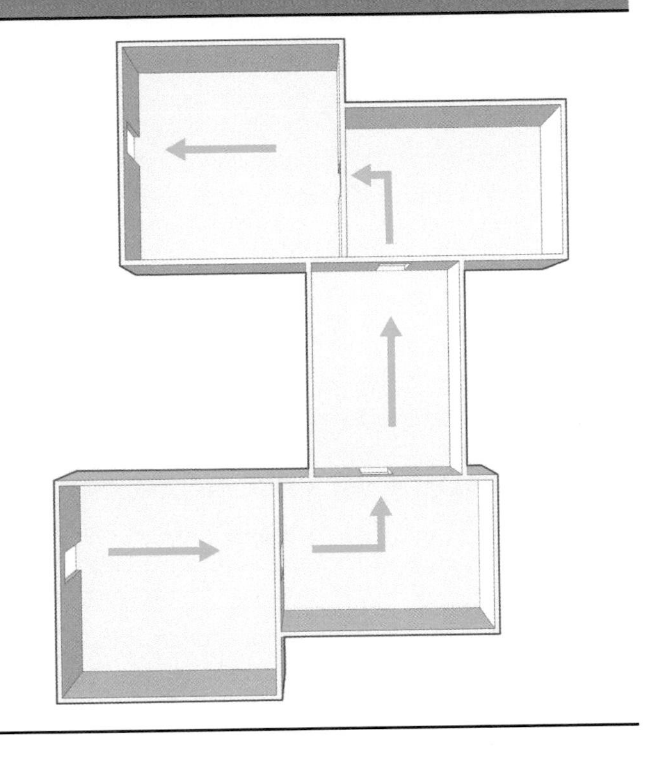

Less straightforward circulation between rooms can lead to creative loops and strategic positioning. It does, however, lose the relationship from part to whole. The gameplay through the level is required to help the player as they can no longer rely on the ability to keep moving forward as affirmation of their wayfinding. If employed without follow through or intention, it can lead to a lack of direction or momentum. In some ways the bland baseline layout performs better than the modular layout if left without direction.

> *Often open world or first person shooter games will fall victim to the endless hallway trope. Presumably if you've played a mission that was boring, this may have contributed.* Skyrim *relies heavily on its polish and art direction in caves and houses. When breaking away from the expectation of a linear path, it often does not afford the wayfinding or incentivizing tools to help players orient themselves. This could be as simple as organizing colored lights consistently throughout the game, using orange for public spaces and blue for private spaces.* Bioshock *leverages this tactic by allowing you to hack machines and change their light from red to green. The light reflects off of the water and allows the player to keep track of their path without*

forcing the player to enter the room again. Portal *also leverages this by priming the player while a single path forward is available. Orange lights illuminate the early portions of the test chamber, where blues are introduced near the exit. As the levels become less confined, the same tactic is leveraged to direct the player to explore in the right direction without limiting them to a linear path.*

From a city planning level, every piece of land has a development plan for what the maximum buildable area is for that location. Cities also introduce neighborhood specific rules tailored by community representatives. This allows the city to control and develop infrastructure to the correct capacity. These are available to the public and can be leveraged by game designers in open world applications especially. If you were to recreate or change an existing city, these documents can give you a good idea of what went into curating that location thus far. As mentioned in the context and vernacular chapters, these patterns drive a lot of the look and feel of a city. Supposing rules for a game environment pays off in very subtle ways, helping orient and direct people passively. Mimicking or subverting familiar locations allows designers to curate the atmosphere and set artists up for success when detailing at a finer level.

Shapes and orientations of walls have straightforward repercussions. Organizing spaces to provide minimum circulation distances are a primary function of space design. Walls can also be leveraged to make spaces appear more open without adding square footage. By using tools other than adding area, it's easy to find new ways to differentiate spaces from each other. Similar to web design, spaces can realistically only become so large, at a certain point a hierarchy must be established. Scaling rooms and buildings as they relate to narrative importance or societal importance can also provide a lot of direction for a team. At a certain point, you must work backward from what the largest room can feasibly be and scale spaces in relationship to that. In Kingdom Hearts 3, we see this problem occur almost immediately, an important space becomes too big to navigate through the typical means of conveyance. The extended volume doesn't provide performative or visual clarity to the level. In Breath of the Wild, we see Hyrule Castle use scale to its advantage. Each room leading up to the final fight is tall, but the dimensions of the room are typically narrow. The final boss fight happens in a massive and spacious volume.

A major consideration of building design lies within cost. The least expensive way to enclose space is creating an extruded box. Many would think to look to complexity for interest. Eisenman's House experiments are dedicated to how odd it would be to see a perfect cube building. This indicates an abstract desire for perfection. It also is a very subtle way to draw a lot of attention.

As far as design planning goes, our workflows are not entirely different. Long story short, we have large budgets and do not generate the funds to build what we design. We have teams that help cover roles from design architect to specifications writer. Architects write Ikea instructions for contractors. Better instructions yield lower construction costs.

We also suffer from a similar problem of "Too many cooks"—everyone in our field is wildly creative. The lead designer must work to ensure that the team can have success working within the given framework. This can't be ensured, but it can be facilitated. For instance, reducing unique solutions. If a series of geometries serve as a variety of corner conditions, the team is more successful overall.

Designing the playable area to have interactivity and engagement in areas that look accessible based on flatness and articulation is important. Using level of detail and game mechanics, level designers can create an expectation for players. Providing some indication of whether or not the player should continue looking in a certain area or move can start in grey boxing. Even before props or lights direct people in or around obstacles.

Providing strategic advantages to more challenging to access areas can make for compelling gameplay. *Super Mario Brothers* champions this, while reaching higher and higher platforms, it not only provides secret areas and power ups, it is also functionally opposite of falling through the level. The top and bottom portions of the screen are not equivalent in that way, just as left and right are not equivalent.

> Breath of the Wild *leverages a seamless constant opportunity to climb up very high and glide to a distant location. It's built into the kit which Link always has available to him. BOTW also allows horses to be captured and called at certain locations. Both of these vehicles allow the player some agency to choose to move quickly or slowly, depending on their preference and current quest.*

Sekiro references geography and city design from fishing towns. To a large extent, the character lacks a lot of accessibility challenges that would inhibit choosing this design for a space. At times it leverages the sectional values of this as well. It does, however, take one deviation from the typology. The accessibility of the character movements is tied to the swing of his longsword, this widens the proportions of certain pathways if they double as staged combat areas.

References from suburban towns are tailored for car scaled travel and will force frustrating gap between proximity and game time spent in transit versus speed of character being unnaturally fast/relying on quick travel.

> Tribes *most notably has beautiful sweeping landscapes, but without the mechanic to slip and slide down them. Imagine walking through that space, it would take forever and be quite boring. The most advantageous path would always be a straight line, with* Tribes *your path finding skills are required to improve impact.* Tribes *leveraged a speed skiing mechanic, that created a more preferred path of travel than simply a straight line between bases. While not a lot of obstacles were generated for these maps, the terrain was finely tuned to create flanking opportunities, stealthy low key routes, and well traveled assault-focused paths.*

Virtual urban environments typically prioritize a general look and layout but do not fill it out completely as shown below.

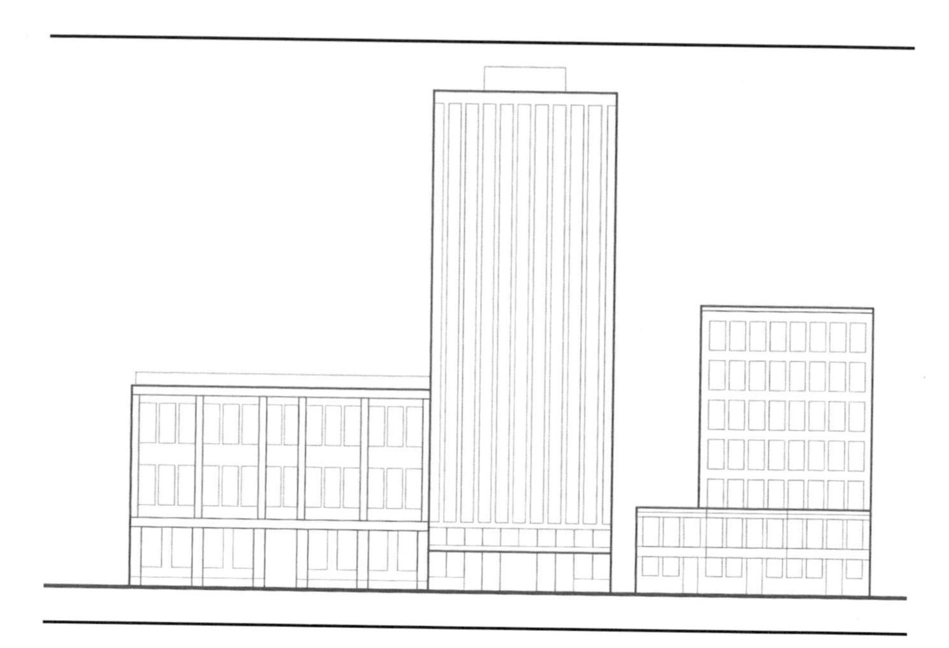

From there, the decision point is where to locate interactive nodes. Knowing how long a task should take is the first step to making spatial decisions. Often games encounter a scalar mismatch of quickly moving a pedestrian through a large city in a way that feels comfortable from a couch. One solution is to treat locations as sets, providing pathways between interactive locations as shown below.

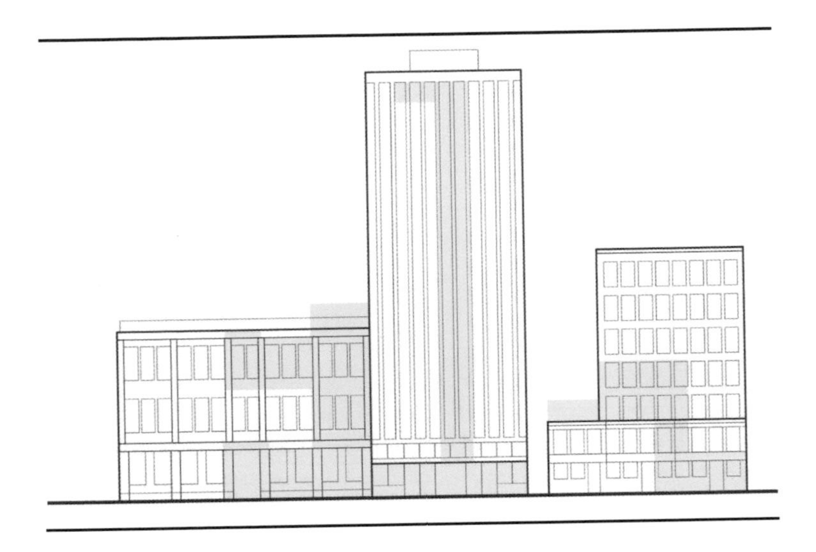

This often forgoes spatial relationships between spaces and can make interior and exterior spaces mutually exclusive. Another solution is to condense interactive elements to a street, plaza, or mall. These can leverage set like proximity, relying on minimaps and sets to resolve distance as shown below.

> Persona 5 *leverages "districts" with an interactive minimap. This affords atmospheric indoor and outdoor experiences associated with each location. This also affords indoor and outdoor sets for interactions at a location. The atmosphere of the location is paramount to the narrative. Vignettes are set up as a "slice of life" for that moment in time. This allows the geographic location and circulation to serve as a reference but not a major story telling point.*

If proximity cannot be resolved through spatial planning alone, the solution may be providing vehicles. This of course has impacts on the city itself. American cities, for instance, have a variety of reactions to the car. Las Vegas, LA, and a variety of suburbs design for vehicular circulation primary to pedestrian circulation. Cities which embrace the new urbanist movements build for bicycle and pedestrian traffic with minimal lanes dedicated to vehicular transit.

> *The environments created for* Titanfall 2 *are so unique to that game because of the wallslide. Creating a level where the player was given 100% agency to vertical movement and granted limited agency of horizontal movement is bold. More commonly, 3D games will use elevators or platforms to lift the character as opposed to translate them. This choice accentuated the futility of the pilot without the titan, allowing a critical plot point to resonate with the player at a more personal level.*

When pieces of a building can immaterially be sorted into blocks and understood as a repeating pattern, occupants can more predictably comprehend hierarchy. Modules become important as a means of determining how spaces can relate to each other. The actual ratio is about 1.61. This miraculously also describes the visual availability for an average human's sight line over a building.

"Intelligibility" or prioritizing visuals allow the player to navigate with intention [whiteboard test].

Boundary has a massive job in level design, it is the rails for the roller coaster the player is about to go on. It's the invisible hand that ensures your player stays immersed in the gameplay. Unlike a roller coaster, it gets added onto and torn apart through trial and error in testing. Presumably this process works pretty well as is, but there are things designers can do to afford more control even late in development stages as they learn more about the way the gameplay and narrative unravel.

Level geometry can disguise load points, funnel combat, and prevent backtracking to name a few. Action games often leverage this for combat. *Destiny 2* (2017) leverages massive set pieces and artwork to disguise a somewhat linear path of travel. Using scraps of metal for available cover and choke points, the game encourages a natural progression forward to the next area. Forests provide a natural buffer between the playable and unplayable area while allowing the space to feel open. By using distractions to keep the player in the intended area, the boundary is not often tested.

Marvel's Spider-Man (2018) had the exact opposite strategy, make one massive map with diminishing resolution on details as you get further from the scripted missions. The designer used zoning as a means of mapping out neighborhoods and objectives.

Developing Solutions

As with any spatial design, theories and visuals alone will not make your level work. Even if a building is a masterpiece of architectural design, it may perform poorly as a level. Designing spaces that work with gameplay patterns could lead to a much more productive round of critique and problem solving. Ultimately, levels work well when they facilitate gameplay and create a sense of place. Designers should be cognizant of how important the function is to the success of the space. Designing levels that acknowledge player mobility, skill level, and narrative can make a level more compelling or immersive. The art director also risks losing clarity as designers will need to develop unique solutions on a case by case basis instead of relying on a system.

> *The same is true for built architecture, if expectations for the design don't consider material constraints from the beginning. A lack of planning can make its way into the realized work. It's incredibly challenging to gracefully integrate downspouts or depths of materials late in the design process. Architects use gridlines and patterns to demonstrate where seams should land as the project gets more developed. Developing systems and patterns to resolve "seams" can also reduce abandoned work.*

Spatial relationships give the player more control over the opponent. High ground has obvious tactical advantages, providing a vantage point from a surveillance perspective. Entering into a room in the center of a wall requires a visual sweep, in that sense going into a room offers a moment of suspense and opportunity for unknown. Providing a preview into the room or entering offset provides a sense that the player can "know" the room. Making a space relatable to a domestic environment feels safer than a large public space.

Humans will be wary of unfamiliar spaces. All of this being said, it is fun and intriguing to subvert some of these notions. False walls and sight lines can undermine the survey a player does after entering a room. Small spaces offer reprieve from danger typically, but could also be a trash compactor.

Another way to experiment with this is by paying attention to what players create. Games solely revolving around giving players the tools to control their spaces provide some capacity to study this. Minecraft a means of attaining "safety" and allowing players to manipulate materials and land to best achieve this goal. Digging into the earth is a great way to reduce travel distance between material gathering expeditions. This creates a subversion of the desire for a height advantage. When players must choose between two viable solutions based on preferred gameplay, it creates a memorable and engaging experience. Giving the player agency and control over these choices creates a responsibility for the player to look for better solutions and builds interest in the game.

> Subnautica *leverages a crashed shelter and minimal resources to demonstrate the opportunity for shelter. It provides a clear gap between what is given to the player versus earned through gameplay. Building up over time, the player can create a new base. Functionally, materials require more resources to harvest. As a result, the requirement for a larger base, more storage, and more tools creates a progression and boundary for the game alleviating that responsibility from the environment itself. Similarly, studios build modular pieces for level designers to create a variety of spaces while maintaining the atmosphere. Unfortunately, this can lead to repetitive gameplay.*

Often cut scenes will be used to help players realize if they're in a safe space or not if it's ambiguous. Bosses and enemies with predictable attacks also help the player understand where a more advantageous location could be. Progressively more challenging moves can then be introduced which disrupt the expectation to encourage a variety of play styles. Geometry can be used to also help players see trends by suspending frantic moments without pulling them out of gameplay.

Geometry can also be used to get a different vantage point. *Assassin's Creed* is known for this discovery mechanic, revealing information about an area after getting to the tallest spire around. *Breath of the Wild's* glider mechanic incentivizes to climbing to the high vantage point. The utility of this method of travel encourages casual exploration.

Multi-player and arena maps are a little tougher, because balance becomes less predictable. While simple, *Team Fortress 2* mastered a variety of symmetrical and asymmetrical maps with pinch points, relying on team strategy and individual gameplay to overcome a well-located defensive line. This forces team composition changes mid game and encourages the use of the best tool for the job rather than a single favorite character. Games like Destiny have arena maps with combat stages, providing sniper sight lines as a mechanism to move the fight around. A massive natural barrier is also often employed to allow a fight or flight response to outside fire.

6

Form

The first understanding of architecture is "massing," developing programmatic elements (room functions), height, and envelope (exterior boundaries). Determining the general shape of the building is, predictably, the first step of designing a building. Many practicing architects subscribe to the design mentality that form follows function. Architects can rely on functionality as a viable foundation for good design.

Evaluating the role of boundaries in games can shed some light on how quickly architectural design comes into game design. Levels in *Duke Nukem* (1996) simply define the boundary of the playable area, showing textures and depicting an extrusion of the floor plan. This functions entirely as a boundary, using materials only to depict a basic understanding of an approximation of a location. This relies heavily on the player to use their imagination. A few years later, game environments could graphically depict illustrations of architecture. These function as a backdrop to give a more prescriptive understanding of the location the designer is trying to depict. Shortly after we see architecture is being used to fill in narrative gaps for players. It also begins to indicate advantageous strategies for the upcoming obstacles. Since then, we have seen many sophisticated combat games leverage level design for strategic purposes.

Massing

Massing is the first means of testing the merit of a design before investing a lot of time into fleshing it out. Allowing the onus of facilitating gameplay to become a core portion of the level design is a great way to critique massing or greyboxing of a level. By forcing the massing to address usability issues, it front loads the design process to a more malleable version of the level as well. In architecture, we leverage consultants during "schematic design" to tackle problems in a similar way. Bringing on a general contractor to review a moment in the design well before it absolutely needs to work can alleviate false assumptions and miscommunications while redesign costs are low.

Inherently all spaces, over time have developed values and cultural identity. Understanding these existing biases can help build concepts quickly. The first organization considers how time relates to structure. Post and beam is the simplest organization and serves dual purpose. It visually depicts the way forces flow through a building. It can break down the scale of the building. Deviation from this norm was provided through steel. Concealed structure, allowing the design to become ambivalent opened the door a new type of architecture. Our most recent paradigm shift is still in process, the digital revolution. Now with CAD assisted calculations, any number of shapes can be fabricated. Prior to that moment, most curvilinear things imagined were ideal. Not a ton of blobs happened before computers. With increased fidelity between design, engineering, and fabrication, architects can be responsible for much more complex curves. Steel paved the way for new spatial organizations.

These are laid out by Corbusier in his five points of modern architecture as shown below using Corbusier's Villa Savoye as a visual reference. Organization of space became significantly less dependent on the structural system. Interior design could begin to create relationships and reliance on spaces instead of structure alone.

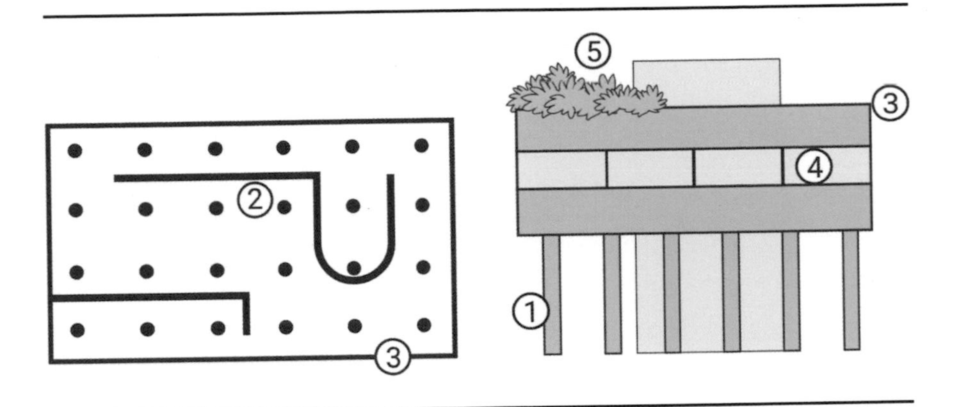

1. Pilotis: Slender concrete columns without top or bottom ornamentation
2. Free Plan: Columns reduce reliance on stacking walls for support
3. Free Facade: Bearing walls no longer determine glazing locations
4. Ribbon Window: Windows can span laterally and light rooms more evenly
5. Roof Garden: Flat concrete roofs on residential homes can be leveraged to grow plants.

A perfect sphere is teased in the form of domes. As it formally does not have much function as an envelope, it was the most logical stopping point. When large enough it is hard to define size or boundary with perspectival vision. Relative to our earth, it is revered as "heavenly." When constructed, ends up requiring facets, either like an icosahedron (like a soccer ball), ribbed (like an orange), or geodesic (triangles tessellated around the surface). Most recently spheres have become more organically assembled with catenary curves.

While it seems as if it'd be familiar enough, cubes are also somewhat mystical. Holding the plan and section to the same dimensions is actually less common and more unsettling than you'd think. Cubes hold importance when separated or pulled apart from a main form, per Corbusier's dovecotes at La Tourette or Gehry's Familian House. It also holds as an origin for paper architects like Peter Eisenman's House series. This is a wildly simple way to create an "unnerving" or "mystical" experience in a way that operates below the level of consciousness.

Additionally, a rectangular volume with its length 1.61 times as long as its width creates another ideal shape. The golden ratio describes the rectangular geometry created by tiling squares of Fibonacci numbers. This creates an ideal space but, of course, may throw off your grid.

Interior of building does not need to be smaller than exterior.

This is going to be a weird chapter. To provide some context, buildings have an inseparable bond with the human range of motion. In virtual environments, game designers have control over the range of motion of the character and by proxy the player. As a result, this chapter lists dimensions, with the understanding that they are only applicable to humans.

Taking a completely different route, level designers also have the capacity to create geometry that is not absolute. *Bioshock's* Fort-Frolic featured plaster splicers that came to life off screen. The same tactic can be leveraged for environments, creating a non-permanent location. This has the potential to be deeply unsettling to players, creating a room that cannot be cleared or quantified, using shaders to create false perspectives and swap in new geometry. Early examples can be seen in *Super Mario Bros.* with the ghost levels. Creating an expectation to progress by completion is not necessarily the case. Subverting an expectation can be incredibly powerful, repetition or subtle deviation introduced at a point where the player is becoming accustomed to a rhythm can have a huge impact.

Spatial mapping allows people to survey and create 3D understanding of the 2D image that they're seeing. When the cognitive map gets disrupted or disoriented, it triggers upset and alert feelings. Even something as simple as changing the paintings or textures on a wall can merit the crucial doubletake.

Relationships

Combining multiple volumes together becomes the next step, finding opportunities to compare and build relationships between spaces. While there is no requirement to marry the interior to the exterior of a virtual structure, there are benefits. The act of choosing an envelope and filling it with spaces forces the designer to adhere to some rules of efficiency and scale. It also reveals patterns as the spaces exhibit similar or differing requirements. A single massive room allows the floor plan to be visualized and embellished by the ceiling plan. Notably, this design typology is often used as an assembly space or place of worship. Volumetrically, extruding the shape of a cross creates transepts. A major and minor axis can be formed based on how tall each ceiling is. From there importance can be derived from the order of overlapping spaces.

Considering the module of the material may also provide some clarity to locating architectural elements. Frank Lloyd Wright heralded this as a primary justification for the literal dimensions of rooms. Proportion was made available on a sliding scale of modules.

Forms don't need to be complex or clad in gold to be impressive. Scale can mystify and create a sense of wonder even if just slightly exaggerated from the built environment. Making a large, unarticulated form can indicate power, articulating a small room can demonstrate wealth and cultural prosperity. It also runs the risk of grotesque escalation, becoming imperceptible or numbing as structures reach a certain scale. Virtual architecture certainly has this advantage over traditional architecture, scaling without fear of structural or fiscal repercussions.

Atriums provide space much larger than can be accessed by occupants, gesturing an importance to the volume beyond the minimum requirement. Game environments have similar opportunities available. Ironically, contemporary buildings have moved away from human scale articulation as a result of more consistency in large manufactured materials. The necessity to break up facades is no longer as high of a concern now that large swaths of materials won't waver or oil-can. This is a bias introduced solely by material constraints, of course, something that digital designers have absolute control over. Labor cost is also fractionally impactful, once a texture is generated, it can span as far as imaginable, with additional cost to computing at most.

Disneyland's architecture undergoes a challenge of seeming appropriately scaled but also accommodating a large occupancy load. They achieve this by scaling the facade up, especially the details, and primarily work in plan to hide the largeness of a space. This allows Disney designers to focus primarily on detailing like cornices and eaves to provide a caricature of familiar architecture. Not only does this serve as a tool for helping lay-people to recognize architectural styles, it also provides a lighthearted approach to an otherwise weighty topic. This prevents the structure from being compared to the original in a literal sense. This is key to taking artistic license to deviate from accuracy and believability. This maintains the brand of the company which relies on viewers to suspend disbelief when given an ounce of truth. This allows the fantasy to also call on familiar tropes that evokes imagination in older audiences.

Providing openings in massing affords sightlines. Designing a system to safeguard these through design can be helpful. Planning major form moves around openings can help deliver impact and framing to dramatic moments. When looking to find ways to draw attention to a space, inviting a new quality of light in or providing a visual connection can entice your player to pay attention. Carving away nearby surfaces is a great way to draw attention.

Creating sight lines actually happens through reduction more often than addition. In built environments, indoor openings come at the cost of additional structure and fire safety. Looking to built structures as reference may yield overly conservative results. Blocking out openings is more effective earlier than later in development. Finding opportunities for voids after planning spaces is challenging and is often causes more ripple effects.

> *Many outdoor exploration games leverage the contrast of solid and void in ruins, temples or caves.* Tomb Raider *games use natural light to contrast the circulation leading up to a focal point. This allows the heavy feeling of mass and weight to build up as the player navigates through spaces unchanged and unvisited. When the player reaches the destination, a larger space with light, fostering new growth, draws a stark contrast.*

Urban spaces can benefit from open spaces as they can provide places to gather. Parks, plazas, and squares allow interactions to happen organically. The success of the spaces is determined by their ambient activity and ease of surveillance. Access to natural light is not only beneficial for any plants trying to grow there, it also provides visibility. In North America, we get more sun exposure from the south and tend to be mindful of this when locating outdoor gathering areas.

Well-designed urban environments are filled with excellent demonstrations of open space. Haussmann's design for Paris is entirely designed around sight lines. This reinforces a sense of place and character for the city and as a result is quite memorable. It also functions as an orientation tool as well. The Uffizi Gallery's courtyard leverages the wings of the building to shade the open space below. While it still gets enough sun to support life in the courtyard, the light bathes the interior facades throughout the day.

Interior openings, atriums, visually connect multiple floors. Often leveraged in lobbies, atriums create a memorable first impression. Creating these spatial connections can help orient occupants as well. Using ceiling heights to codify spaces especially during an entry sequence can curate an experience.

> *Louis Kahn's Phillips Exeter Academy Library uses a massive void in the center of a heavy structure, is open to the "stacks" and additionally provides large circular voids in the concrete for additional light to come through the structure*

More challenging still is creating the desire or memory of something there. Eisenman's house II does this in an incredibly sophisticated way that could be missed if not actively tailoring the expectation. The ford foundation does this rather simply, by building out a garden before enclosing the building with an exterior glass wall. This move creates a feeling that the floors were carved instead of just not making it there in time.

In gameplay this has been done in some incredible ways. God of War uses destruction as a narrative reason for the player to imagine the void as a scar.

Proportion

Some of the most notable architecture in our canon derives from pulling proportions that worked into projects into a new context. Rowe remarks that architects rely on their ability to "extract from historic and current precedents a formal common denominator—the quality they recognized as correct composition,"[1] "proper character does not necessarily accompany the securing of good composition."

As buildings are incredibly expensive to make, usability is paramount to the space allocation of a building. Proportions begin with what is usable then carve and expand to see how spaces can become individually significant. While this may not be such a necessity for virtual buildings, a single lab room may be the cause of putting a whole campus into a game, there are still some things we could learn from this.

Environments correspond to the occupants using them. For an example of this see a variety of bird nests. The same can be said about humans versus the playable characters in games. Architects rely on codes and rules of thumb for human environments and may require some scaling based on your application. Knowing why we use these givens could shed some light on the ways to adapt concepts to best fit your application.

Primarily, codes help architects determine the absolute minimum dimension required for safe uses, including exit in case of fire. This dictates an astounding amount of the design that you see in the built environment day to day. This standardization empowers architects to provide barrier-free, or handicap accessible, spaces. These numbers are created using humans as a scale: reach height, width, and accessibility all factor in.

[1] He says many things in this chapter—it is challenging to look back and consider any portion of our profession "making no overt display of bias," but he does thoroughly believe that proportion can lead to more pleasing architecture. Mathematics of an Ideal Villa p 60.

Any dimensions mentioned in this book will need to be scaled to your player, for ease of communication. Ideally, this will provide you a benchmark to compare with familiar places. The primary benefit of finding your game's scale compared to the built environment is leveraging and understanding primary sources of information.

If the height of a room is meant to imply the strength of the boss inside of the area, that relationship can use the whole game to build up to the climax. If uncoordinated, you may end up with an underwhelming final battle for your primarily combat driven game. When designed properly, it can be used in lieu of directional arrows and narration.

One challenge in scaling a set piece or level elements is simply the boundary available based on character mobility and scale. The function of determining how interactive elements and set pieces are scaled in advance allows the team to create work that ties the entire game experience together a little more cohesively. Identifying visual or spatial hierarchy from the beginning can also help with time management. Scaling time spent designing environments in proportion with the amount of time the player is expected to spend in a space or narrative impact. Architects prioritize high quality materials in high visibility spaces in order to make more of an impact.

> Titanfall 2 *introduces a level where the player must navigate a level as a bipedal human after piloting a titan. The level is titan scaled, pulling design languages from hangers and factories. The discrepancy challenges the player to overcome challenges to save your companion despite the scalar difference. This not only builds a logical correlation for the player and character to have the same desire, it also is designed to create an emotional impact on the player.*

Architects design for human occupants in our buildings, reach distances and livable rooms are important. From the most theoretical sense, there is an understanding of human proportions, humanism. Occupants can understand scale better if there are a variety of shapes and patterns which are related to humans. In a more practical sense, rooms that are properly proportioned and scaled for the activities and purposes are more pleasing. In the most precise sense, universally accessible design drives the minimum acceptable size for a space.

Understanding density and proportion can help adjust when adjusting to a new context. Manipulating the scale of a room may be easy when changing its massing, when articulated or detailed, it creates many tiny problems.

Many unique problems are unveiled when supposing a "great hall" 10 times the size of any historical reference.

> *Villa la Rotonda relies on temple detailing scaled to residential sizes. Palladio's experiment created many new details and conditions while trying to match the precedent at a smaller scale. This manipulated the source material into something new and almost unrecognizable from its origin point.*

From time to time architects postulate about what modules humans and buildings share. Corbusier and Vitruvius both famously suppose models of humans studying proportional relationships. Most buildings are assembled by humans which inherently has some capacity to convey the scale of a human transitively. The exception would be buildings with prefabricated elements are almost entirely factory built and are then assembled on-site. As a result of this, many building materials must be movable by humans or machines controlled by humans. Notably, Ancient Egyptians and Romans created works which subverted this notion to pay homage to a hierarchy beyond human scale. Interior spaces are primarily driven by the range of mobility humans have, paying attention to creating barrier-free spaces (wheelchair access being the easiest to identify).

7

Space

For the most part, architecture responds in some way to the ground it stands on. In most cases this is a somewhat immutable property of the design. Views, height, and form are all influenced by the site the building was designed for. Location plays a role in the development of the space the architecture occupies and encloses. Spaces can be captured by walls, landscaping, floors, furniture, and scenes. Its immaterial nature affords relationships between soft and hard boundaries.

The first step of creating this space is working through the motifs and spatial constraints to site the building. Considering how the exterior spaces as a framing element develop the first impressions of the space. A long driveway looking from a worm's eye view gives a heroic look to the building. Descending upon a building can help it feel secure. Assisting in this is the siting of the building. Putting the building on stilts can make it seem heroic with a level approach. Embedding a building into a hill can make it look safe. The interior can also help convey a motif. Large rooms can make a space seem regal. Small spaces with nooks can make a space seem loved and cozy. All of these choices can be layered with colors and materials to heighten the effects. Allowing the form to lay the groundwork for the design choices to come can help everyone work together to achieve a similar goal.

Another key benefit of a good understanding of form is control over circulation. Paths of movement through the building can "direct" experiences. Using sequences and angles, the occupant's impressions of the space can be curated to some extent. Allowing circulation to fall out of sync with the form and motifs of the building can lead to lackluster payoffs to otherwise well designed spaces.

Bioshock's *exterior corridors were used to great avail, it perfectly depicts the dichotomy between what the designers wanted it to be versus what it ended up being. The corridors are the glass tubes which extend past the envelope of the structure and into the ocean. Considering the intended perception, defiance physical bounds. This plays up the zeitgeist of a culture looking to demonstrate exceptional engineering, architecture, and design. Providing such an expansive view of rapture showcased this achievement. For the player, stumbling upon rapture after its peak, there is a different perception. This same space served to demonstrate how far the culture had fallen. It visualizes the gravity of being stuck under the ocean and the peril that befell the city as a result of its hubris. All of this is passively afforded by its circulation.*

Virtual spaces also respect boundaries differently. Primarily the separation can be a single plane. The boundary keeps the player in the playable space. In some cases even creating a playable space that is the moment of the outside constantly with links to interior spaces. Barriers prevent access whether it's literally blocking or separating spaces.

Through Exterior Spaces

Controlling the organic environment has been a human fascination for thousands of years. The design that goes into curating virtual exterior environments is wildly different than that of reality. There is no step to creating wilderness. The concept of designing wilderness and respite is unique to virtual mediums. As a result the grooming curation of both natural and manmade spaces falls on the shoulders of the designer.

Typically, gardens, landscapes, and parks require consideration of the ecosystem that is being created. Pathways break up swaths of planted material and can form patterns or develop organically. Gardens hold many narrative opportunities due to their depiction of time passing. The regular play between permanent and seasonal features is unique to landscape architecture.

Gates have the opportunity to call out a path as preferred or intended. They also do not require a wall to have an impact. Passing any threshold can affect the player as shown below.

Often, players can be directed through areas with lights and barackades. Inspiring movement in a certain area using gates can build suspense, become a place-making tool, can be used to tell a story about the supposed path finder leading them through the area. Alternatively, it can still be used to apply shaders or trigger events. A nonverbal indicator that a large fight may be approaching can be primed and conditioned. Symbolically, classical architecture uses colonnades to build up the importance of the threshold. Romans even had a deity dedicated to gates—Janus. Triumphal arches, for instance, commemorate the beginning and celebrate the victory of a battle.

Chinese gardens often use framing to build layers in small spaces, making them appear larger. The Humble Administrator's Garden in Suzhou employs a variety of materials scales and canvases. The layout creates thresholds to announce the entry into a vignette or garden, as shown below, functionally providing punctuation at the end of each theme. Thresholds and gates are fairly prevalent in gardens. Gates don't necessarily need to be a barrier, they can also denote intended path of travel. They are a kind of visual guide, indicating transitions.

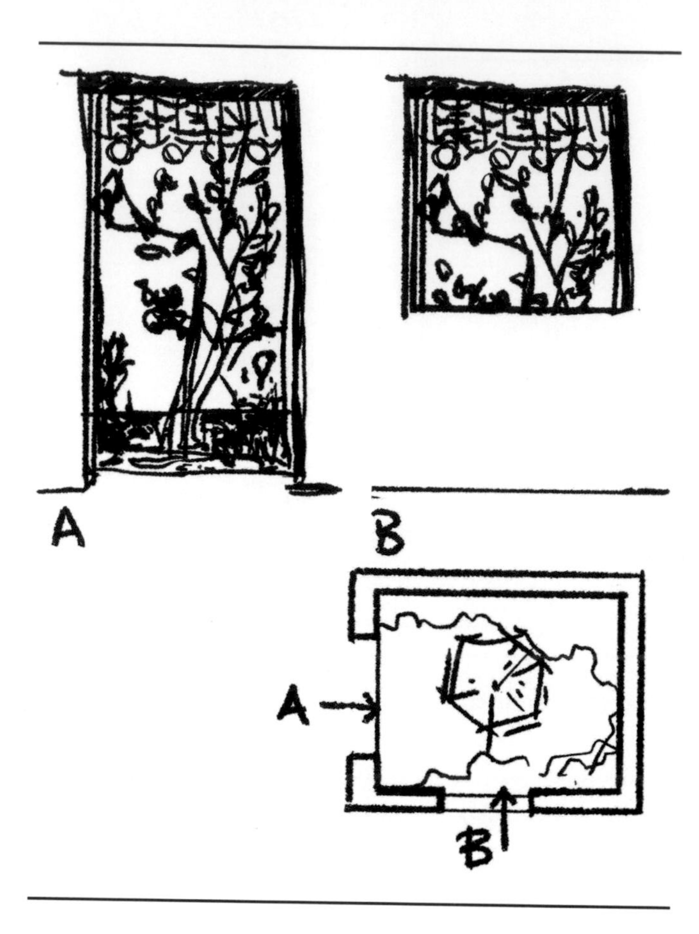

The action of passing through a threshold is actually fairly uncelebrated in games. They're quite often disguising load points or triggers for cut scenes. As a result, many games haven't sorted out how to leverage them yet.

In a very literal sense, gates also provide a frame. They can be used to frame or ask the player to compare things inside and outside of the frame. It also asks the player to compare the shape of the frame to the subject, landscape or horizontal; rectilinear or organic. From point of view, POV, A we have a densely packed organic courtyard. Using an opening, the entire landscaping is revealed, the step occurs at the end of the threshold and invites you into the courtyard. From POV B, the courtyard appears to be mostly wall, sparingly populated with branches. From here the space appears short, as if a picture on a wall. Reframing the same scene can build a more robust understanding of an environment. Something as simple as changing the dominant color of the foreground will change the perception of the subject.

Addressing the way that the building sits on the site is quite specific when designing in a city. More rural areas have a wider range of opportunities. Orientation and relationship to the existing topography should match motivations demonstrated elsewhere in the design. If the building is working to leverage natural ventilation, it would make sense for it to leverage the direction of the wind through the site.

You can carve away the land around a building to create a light well, or moat if you're housing a villain. Light wells indicate an importance of natural light at great cost to the client. Moats indicate of course a desire for isolation and control of entry. The entry for these types of buildings require a bridge. Using a bridge to get to an entry draws builds suspense and importance to that area. This can either be used as a project datum or completely subverted to indicate a coldness in the structure.

A building can be embedded in a landscape, providing a look out in one direction and wrapped in landscaping above. This creates a tie to nature as well as functionally cooling the structure, relying on the retaining wall to act as a battery, maintaining a constant temperature day and night. Overhangs and cross ventilation can further cool the space. It has a cave-like quality and can be engaged as such. It can also be used to evoke a feeling of safety. Again, concrete and stone play a large role in the palette because of the capillary action of groundwater. While polyurethane and metal can resist water, a lot of engineering is required to rely on these materials for retaining soil.

At times, planters will be ganged up at the foundation if walking paths are not required along the perimeter of the building. This allows for functional things such as exhaust, drainage, and privacy to be provided in gaps between buildings. It also provides a more graceful security feature to separate public space from private space. This can be used to soften harsh materials, break up larger buildings, or provide direction and wayfinding. These planters can also be used to host fences above, providing the foundation required for a 6-foot-tall privacy screen.

Approach

There are a variety of major and minor design features related to the moment the building visually begins. Arguably, most are related in some way to our desire as architects to keep water out of the building. This is one of those times that a physical constraint overwhelmingly influences form. Above grade, a building can be any material; at grade, a building has to deal with groundwater; below grade, the building must combat the pressure of groundwater.

Some simple knowledge of water infiltration can explain why certain solutions became so prevalent. The primary problem areas for leaks are the roof and the foundation. Roofs, of course, have to deal with rain water, and runoff could compromise the base of a building. Below that, basements must deal with the constant pressure of groundwater, this is typically solved with a drainage mat. This diverts the water around the structure to avoid capillary action when it comes in contact with concrete walls. In short, the primary goal of a structure is to keep out water. And I'm sure you're thinking "Oh a little water is probably fine. It's fine." It's not fine, zero water is fine. Unless it's kept in pipes.

Medieval homes (Figure 7.1) have tackled this one with a stone floor at the ground level, it's typically inset to handle the material change. Modern building materials (Figure 7.2) can have as little as a 6-inch curb before switching materials.

The resilient base is consistent through many styles, transitioning to architectural-grade finishes above. Materials like concrete and stone are

FIGURE 7.1
Medieval Home Design

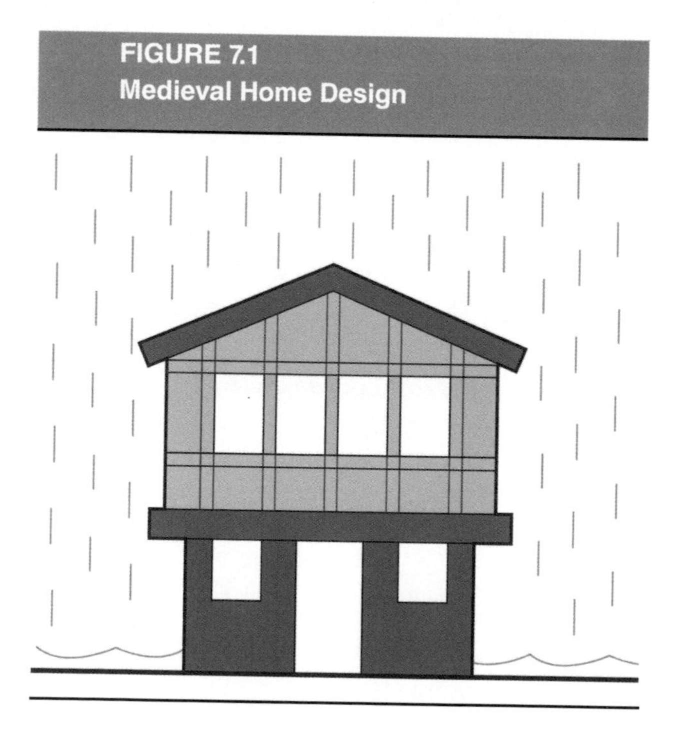

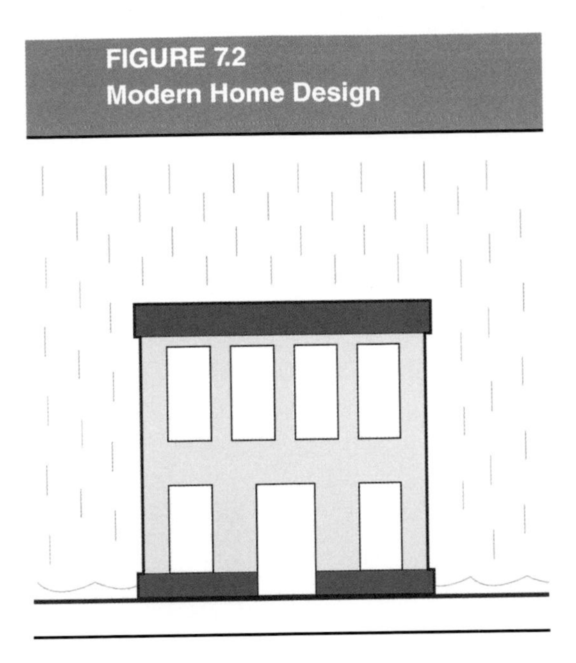
FIGURE 7.2
Modern Home Design

resistant to water, which makes sense for them to commonly hit the ground and protect the above grade walls from moisture. This allows for a transition to a wider variety of materials as shown below.

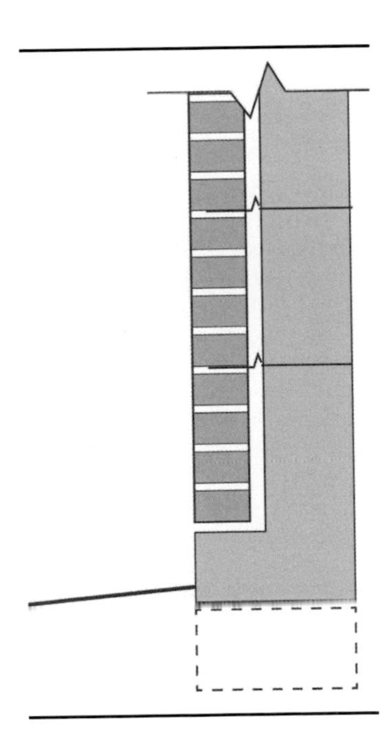

Unfortunately, concrete is super expensive and hard to manipulate in the field. Masonry is pretty durable, and it used to be the only thing actually holding up the exterior walls as shown below.

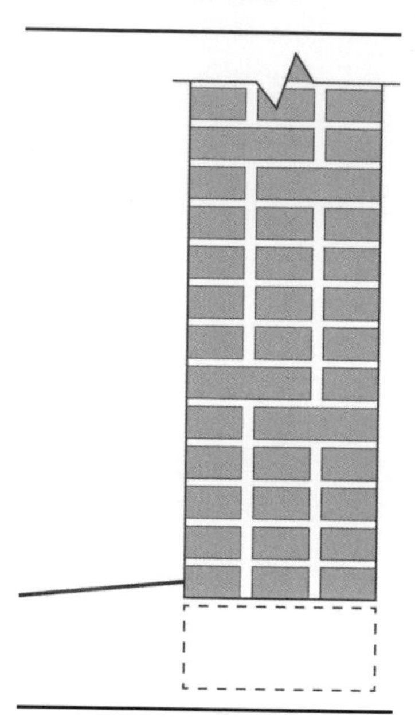

Now we have this weird clip-and-veneer system with an air gap. Due to this change, typically you won't see a brick building literally touch the ground anymore. As far as picking a location for that datum goes, it depends on a few things. Window sills like to be around 3 feet so a Water Table or accentuation of material change gets raised to that level. If the interior is about a smooth transition from interior to exterior, you'll see taller windows and lower curbs.

> *For hundreds of years, the people who were able to afford large buildings had servants which lived on the premises. The exterior of the buildings would indicate this separation of use. Often the Piano Nobile was used to visually separate these two classes. State buildings will often require the public to ascend a flight of stairs to reach the front door. This impresses importance on the entry as well as provides security. So it becomes a vehicle for symbolism, allowing commentary on how the building relates to the land beneath it.*

Climates may influence the base of a building. It shouldn't come as too much of a surprise that more or less rain will change the solution to the waterproofing problem. For the most part, it's advantageous to adapt to the weather and context of the site. Hurricane-prone areas will often have buildings on piers. Venice hosts an array of bulkheads to support the first level of each building. In the desert, cross ventilation is a primary concern, ground floors are much more oriented toward openness. These nuances could help make weather more impactful or more actively tie the design of the building to its context. It also gives you some opportunity to build variety into different cities. In contrast the "International Style" of the 1960s homogenized new buildings. This was a celebration of the opportunity to source and apply materials from all over the world in order to pursue a vision. These mostly rested on an almost mythical field of pilote columns. With the advent of manufactured materials, that are not as hospitable to organic material, came a freedom from design constraints defining the way the building met the ground.

The foundation is the portion of a structure which distributes the weight of the building to bearing soil shown below.

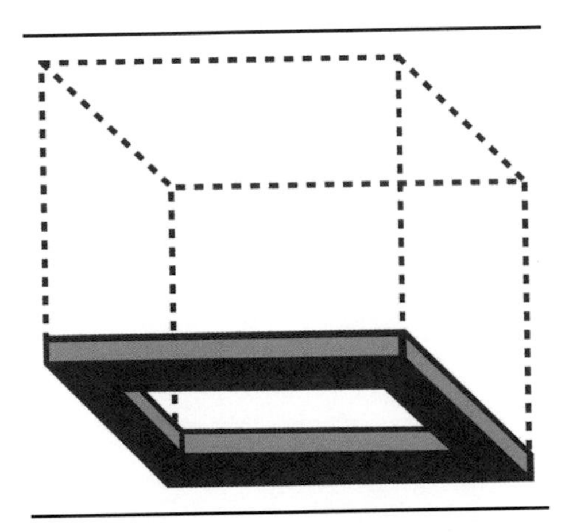

Ideally, these beams will prevent portions of the building from settling unevenly. Most buildings rest on concrete beams called *footers*, which are typically 2 feet wide. From there, the building may require more extreme measures to reach bearing soil. Steel or concrete piles will extend into the ground anywhere from 5 to 60 feet if the bearing soil is not good. This shouldn't impact the above grade portion of the building, but could help if you're looking to place a building onto a non-ground surface.

Contemporary buildings greet the foundation with a concrete curb or stone pediment. The material change in a built structure also triggers a change in thickness for the wall. The thinner material can rest either aligned to the interior, aligned to the exterior, or outboard of the base. This choice can allow the upper portion of the building to look as if it has a rusticated base, has a modern flush look, or inset foundation.

Water table at base is shown below. This is typical. Some accentuation at the base, indicating either the base of the ground floor or entire ground floor. This is visually announces the point at which the building meets the ground. It can symbolically represent respect for the land beneath it.

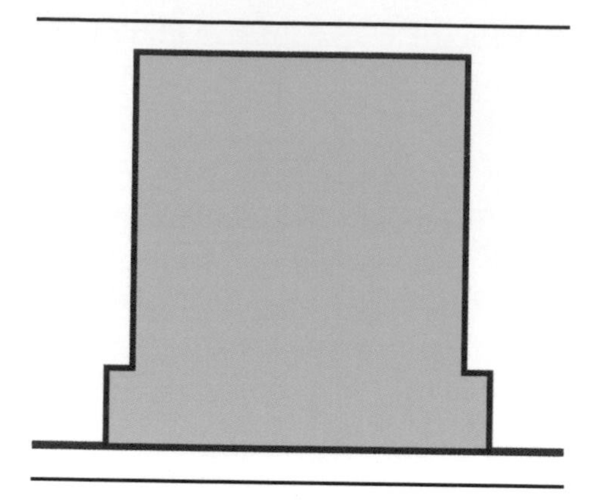

Flush along exterior walls is shown below. There are nuances to achieve flush walls as the material changes toward the base. Pursuing this requires either using more material or creating a fussy detail. The effort required to avoid announcing the base indicates the opportunity to subvert this requirement. Modernism was defined by the subversion of typical building details.

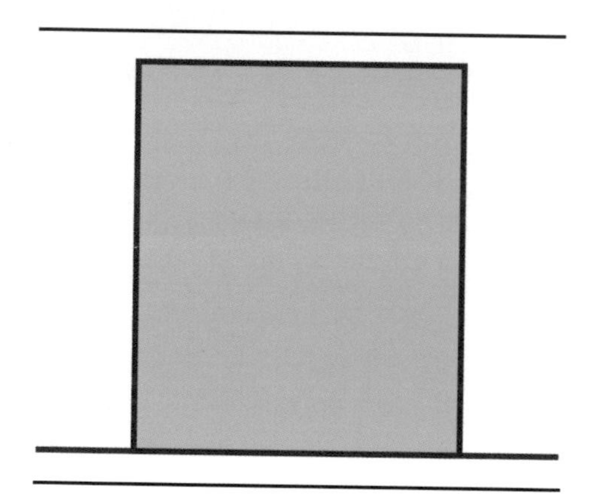

Inset foundation at grade (shown below) creates a variety of challenges depending on the severity. 6″ inches up and 4″ inches out could be enough to get the intended effect. Larger reveals can reduce floor area at grade. The shadow line created by the overhanging facade gives the appearance of floating. Notably the Laban Center Dance uses this shadow to make the facade seem weightless.

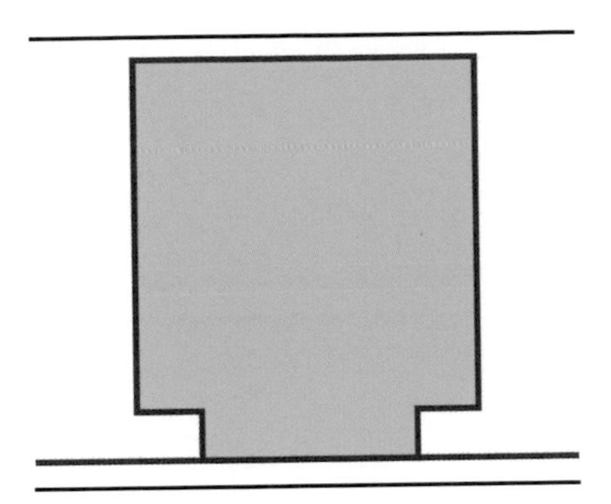

Despite never revealing the ground plane, *The Jetsons* managed to put all of their structures on spokes. The drive at the time was to relate this building to the architecture style of the 1960s and 1970s. It harks back to the optimistic futurist structures of the time. These cartoon illustrations served as shortcuts for well-known buildings at the time.

Walking/tethered is shown below. The implications of making this work may vary upon universe, metals are lightweight and will often give the spindly look with a tone of believability. More brittle like wood or concrete materials would need to rely on frequency to prevent bending in thinner materials. The profile and style of movement will define the feel of this building as much as the material choices. The fleeting interaction with the ground implies a freedom as well as a lack of refuge in any one location.

So inherently a truly floating building as shown below or airship either indicates a lack of accessibility at any point in time. Pneumatic buildings are typically created using multiple cells of gas. Seams will typically be most efficient when symmetrical or tessellated. The launch point creates a new relationship to the ground, indicating a remote support structure at which point the structure takes on a role as stationary. Floating without movement could symbolize nostalgia and "futurism" or vanity and confidence.

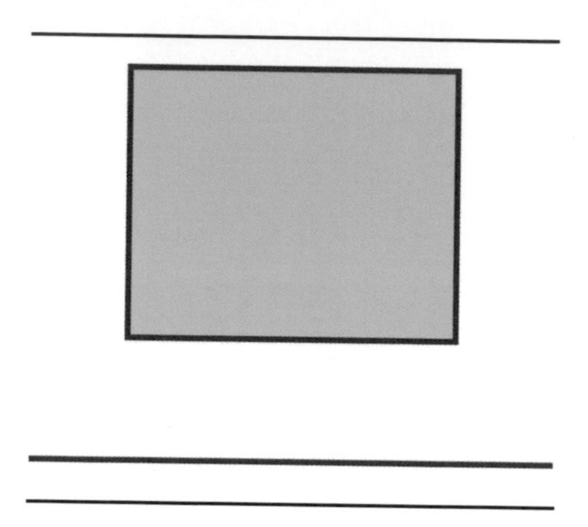

Developing a relationship between the building and the ground the way it meets the ground calls attention to its context. The audience is then able to see where this building fits into the lore provided. The observation of this information is beneficial to the world's cohesion. This now fills in the gaps left by a mysterious main character, a leap.

"Podium" buildings as shown below have more floor area at the base reduce area as it towers up. This is usually a requirement enforced by cities to allow light into streets. This is a typical way to maximize the developable area of a lot. Architects will often find ways to articulate the tower separate from the horizontal portion.

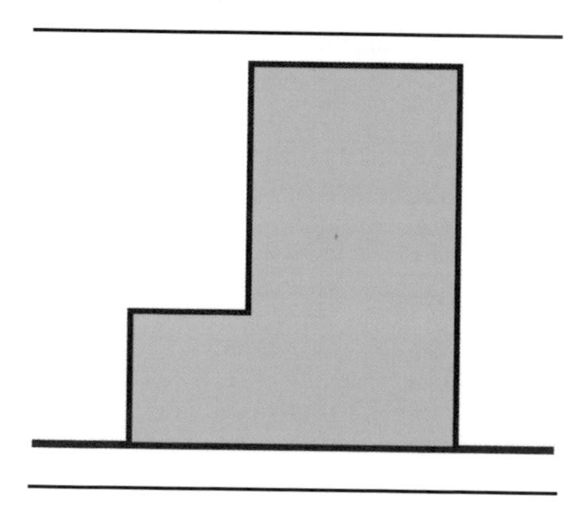

Engaged in hillside, an example of a “walkout basement” is shown below. Many cities will allow for this basement to avoid floor area ratio calculations (free area). Falling water famously joins into the side of a hill. The marriage between built and natural structures can be a platform for complementary interaction or stark differences.

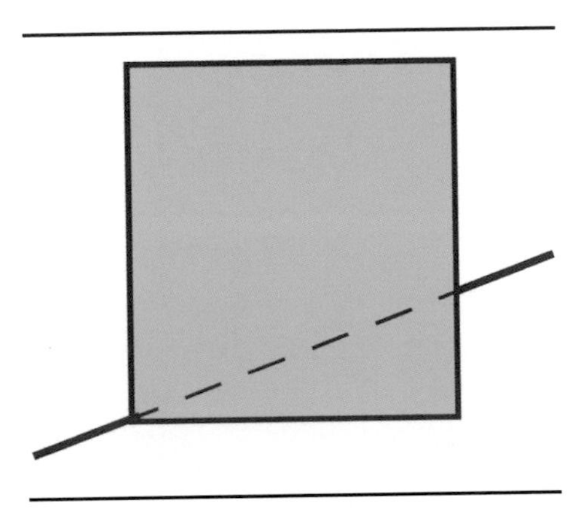

Submerged basement is shown below. Depending on geography, below grade floors can be great places for cellars. Bedrooms require operable windows—so they’ll need light wells to exist completely below grade. By avoiding the option to articulate the exterior at grade, it subverts the typical condition. This could be used to symbolize a continuity through the ground plane.

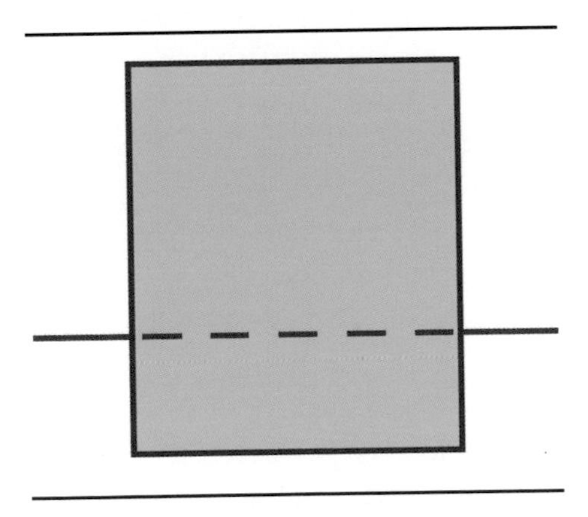

Pilote or raised buildings (shown below) forego a good chunk of the first floor. Often this will be a solution to flooding or supporting functions public passage through the ground floor. Corbusier uses this tactic for Villa Savoye. This can allow the building to read as "aloof" as it creates a new workable ground plane.

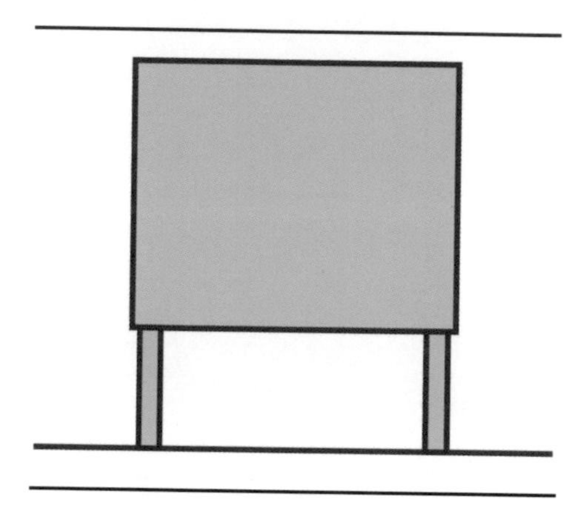

Level designers can curate the perception or impression the building as a "set." The representation of architecture includes lighting and landscaping. In a virtual environment, curation can extend to weather, atmospheric effects, age, color palettes, and styles. Virtual structures don't need to react to physical or temporal constraints. The choice to go with an existing solution has an entirely different set of "pros and cons." Unlike built works, the longevity of virtual architecture is not at risk when deviating from the norm. This encourages a wider variety of approaches to a problem.

The building can also be floated, this is generally achieved by creating a base that has a smaller perimeter than the rest of the building. Appearing to float inches above the ground, a reveal at grade will create the shadow line required. It can also be as severe as resting on piers or columns. The advent of steel sparked an interest in this building type as well as an accessibility of it. Corbusier pioneered this at Villa Savoye noting a paradigm shift. Pilote columns lack base and capital articulation as a means of embodying modern sensibilities.

Concrete or steel can be used to span a structure past a bearing point, most often maxing out at about 6 feet. Cantilevers work like a beam, leveraging only its connection and depth as resistance from overturning. Anything beyond that is of course possible but comes at a greater cost of materials or additional supports or deeper floor plate.

Observation towers use point connections to support the lightweight structure. Finite element analysis provides insight to how forces can flow through a structure.

Movies and pop culture have a tendency to evoke more colorful interactions with the ground. *Howl's Moving Castle* has a fleeting relationship to the ground. Its movement indicates a momentary acknowledgment of the ground immediately beneath the house. This connection with the ground can be related to a foot touching a surface, humanizing it and providing insight to something which is otherwise unrelatable. This detail affords relatability to a moving front door, giving some reference for perception and further thought.

Archigram proposed a similar design for a Walking City, noting a lack of political designation and reverence to history. This forward moving city was a strong recourse to a politically charged world, after the cold war subsided. This desire to depart from a secretive and ultimately dangerous time to a utopia of sorts had inspired many architects.

Through Interior Spaces

A major consideration of the breakdown of interior spaces is circulation. Circulation simply refer to the way people move through a building. It can be purely functional or provide opportunities for gathering as shown below.

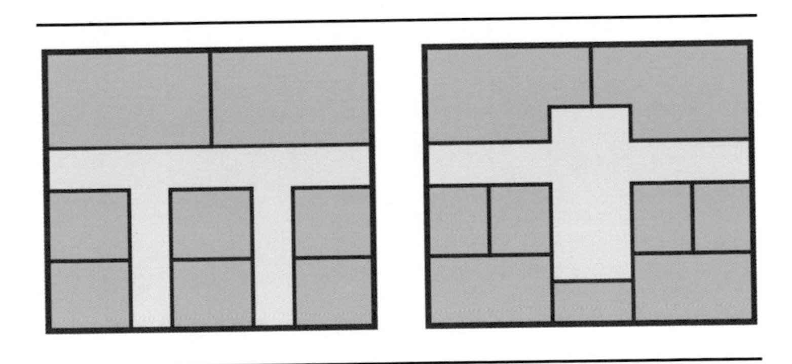

When hallways or circulation spaces for built structures, the goal is generally to minimize it. Functionally, it is not as valuable as a room and adds to travel time if too circuitous.

From the smallest application, an apartment is a small space with the luxury of not needing additional fire separation between rooms. Combining open areas such as kitchens and living rooms as circulation areas is a great way to reduce wasted space as shown below.

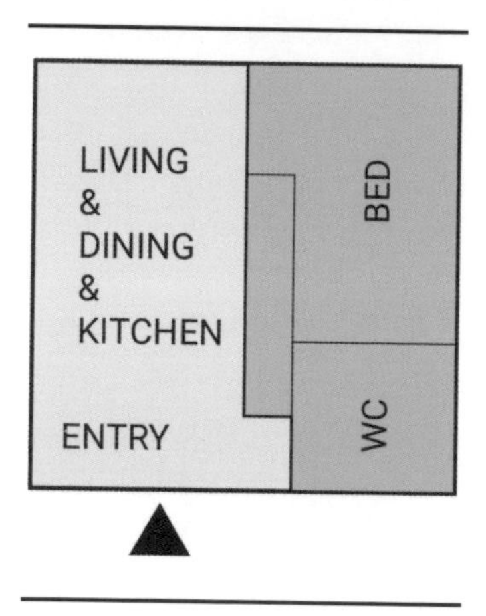

This also serves as a delineation between public and private spaces. Zooming out to the rest of the building, apartment complexes will often have a single hallway lined on either side with units as shown below.

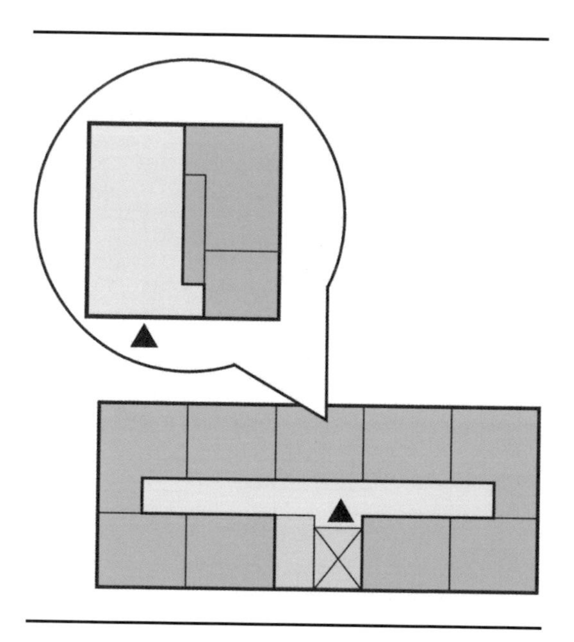

This is efficient for a variety of typologies, single- or double-loaded corridors work well with vertical circulation cores. This also maximizes exterior facing rooms, which provide the opportunity for windows, hospitals, labs, apartments, offices can all benefit from natural daylighting. This primarily works for large buildings that are bar shaped. Single family homes can still benefit from the linear corridor organization. Over the larger area, a standalone home can benefit from a gradient of public to private spaces shown below.

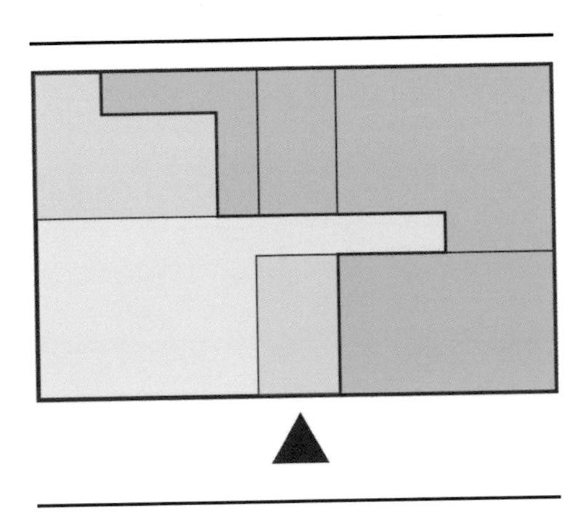

Square or cruciform plans can benefit from centralized circulation as shown below.

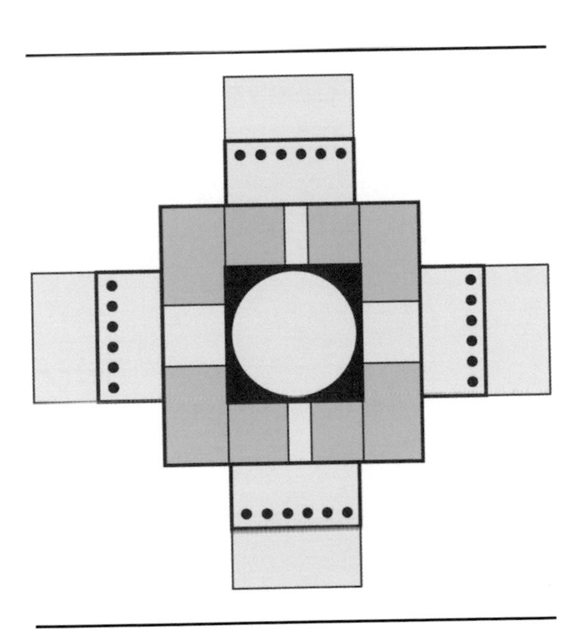

Interior spaces are often characterized with more delicate materials and design moves. Consideration of material quality is much more important as it is closer in proximity to occupants than the exterior of a building often is. The finishes are also interacted with for a longer duration. This tends to favor lower intensity colors with a bold accent rather than bold colors used to create a pattern.

Given these tendencies, direction through interior spaces tends to be consistent through rooms within the same building. Scaling up and down in frequency to afford a spatial flow through the building.

Interior spaces have a tendency to have much more interaction. The finishes are within reach range, lighting is designed to be near the work surface and more frequent, floors are expected to be level. Modern architects can use real-time rendering to vet their interior designs. Humans are already quite skilled at discerning these proportions. Interior design moves don't need to be very loud to have a large impact.

Part III

Materiality

Follow through of motifs can happen through materiality and detailing. These subtle choices are critical to continued immersion. Players may choose to spend anywhere from 10 minutes to 10 hours in a space. Environments can continually add to the experience of a location. Providing a variety of canvases can help solidify the most important threads of a concept.

As previously mentioned, the major difference between art and architecture lies in seams. The breaking point that one material demands may impact other materials. Materials need only concern themselves with how they work as a layer and how that layer is fastened to the structure. The coordination of "stopping places" for materials rests on the shoulders of the architect. From there, everything is a decision point. For a designer of virtual architecture, this could be a major fork in the road for the design process. Are buildings in general "believable" or "fantastic"? Is the player responsible for observing the environment or should it influence them passively?

There are many ways to visualize socioeconomic traits of a neighborhood. Consistency in detailing can help players know what to rely on for additional information. Is it valuable for them to notice that the paving changed from one part of the city to another?

Bioshock leverages art deco details on a streamline modern massing. This gives it a completely new iteration of a familiar style. The details are immediately recognizable as art deco permeated into art and design as well as architecture. The reposition of recognizable graphic styles in new spaces created something between familiar and unfamiliar.

Being wary of the number of influences you put in front of the player is a level of curation only available to game designers. In addition to controlling the entirety of the context of a city, the global illumination, and the people, game designers can also control the way buildings age. Binding your game to a level of detail can resolve a lot of qualitative questions.

Considering how forces, materials, and history impacts built architecture can inspire a wide variety of secondary and tertiary architectural elements. Considering brickwork as a texture is probably the first level, considering how bricks interact with the openings created by windows and doors. Finally, defining the era of the building with either ornamental ties, decorative brickwork, or the way it announces a new material would demonstrate a higher level of architectural detail. From there, landscaping, activation by entourage, or lighting can draw attention to it.

Another interesting distinction revolves around designing to make something memorable or distinctive. As of writing, architects are fascinated with a contemporary understanding of "modernism." Modernism, defined by reductive or clean lines leveraged to demonstrate organization and quality. This clean look is hard to achieve in a built environment as it requires an incredibly skilled architect who is not reliant on their contractor to anticipate conditions. It also requires a high-quality contractor that is able to perfectly follow the drawings as anticipated by the architect. The reduced lines and clean connections demonstrate conditions that other architects may not be skilled enough to anticipate or too cautious to rely on. Over time, through failures, through optimization, supply companies have worked to reduce the liability of using their materials. As a result, we're seeing many buildings attempt these "safe-modern" designs. Allowing small failure points to not result in a complete failure. As a result, I see us approaching a paradigm shift to indicate a less reproducible way to distinguish a building as "memorable." Similarly modernism in game environments, eliminating seams is not impressive—they end up looking "lazy" instead.

8

Dimensions

There's an important distinction between practice and theory for architects. In practice, architectural drawings are legal documents which serve as instructions for general contractors. They're informed by codes, engineers, and client decisions. Theoretical architecture is often designed without cross-disciplinary influences. Either is important for canon, but the theoretical understanding often gets perpetuated through academia. In practice, buildings are entirely reliant on numerical bounds.

Facades in theoretical projects must only concern themselves with composition and context. The primary role of the design is to suppose an opportunity for conveying an idea. This allows the focus to shift primarily to architecture in a pure form, unbiased by constraints. This is valuable as constraints and codes often change, supposing how it affects design is a valuable exercise. These designs are also mindful of crutches—being careful to hold no other parties responsible for architectural expression.

Facades in practice require an incredible amount of precision to design. On the interior, they must accommodate the spacing of rooms. Codes determine how high the sill of an operable window can be and what percentage of the wall must be opaque. Ventilation, cladding, details, openings, all require a numerical system to allow them to coexist on the same facade gracefully. It starts by understanding the linear footage available and separation constraints. From there, the designer must understand which dimensions are flexible and which prefer a modular approach. A good understanding of dimensions can help the designer create patterns for these interacting requirements. Ideally, the facade's design can be another vehicle for the parti while effortlessly affording the expected coordination. If left unresolved, the expected coordination items will disrupt the composition. The requirements related to ventilation and construction are more tangible and will often overrule the more ambiguous requirements for design.

In practice, composition is often safeguarded by gridlines and coordination. Building in flexibility for other disciplines can act as a lightning rod. Communicating patterns and datums through gridlines also allows elements to line up from floor to floor with less effort.

Locating walls and elements precisely is called "dimensioning." This allows the architect to call out where the control point of a wall or structure as well as its distance from a gridline or parent object is. This is primarily used for the contractor but helps during coordination too. Engineers will often look to optimize their solutions and will propose small changes to the architecture to reduce the cross section of a beam or column. Identifying how a wall was located as well as crucial dimensions can help others contributing to the project.

Most buildings are designed with gridlines and all buildings need dimensions to describe instructions to engineers and contractors. Dimensions are the engineering portion of architecture; they provide numerical information and relationships.

Buildings are designed to human proportions. Legally we are required to. Codes help prescribe what is required to serve the most restrictive use case. Architects rely on standards of reach heights, worktop heights, and navigation paths. This is the incredibly obvious if you've ever been to an older city with exterior steps or cramped hallways. If you've ever been somewhere and wondered how a wheelchair would get there, it most likely couldn't be permitted like that today. For your convenience, there is an appendix of "rules of thumb" at the end of the book. By no means are these numbers devoid of biases, but could serve as a valuable reference point.

Architecture, by law, must be accessible. Buildings should be safe and usable for all types of people. Structures built before 1960 did not have this requirement. These are probably noticeable by their stairs or handrails to an ambulatory person. To someone in a wheelchair the architectural shortcomings may be more noticeable, higher thresholds, inaccessible or wildly unusable worktops, uneven floors and flooring.

The best description of this is actually mailboxes. At time of writing, the upper range of reachability is capped by how reasonable it is to expect someone in a wheelchair to not only reach the door but also open with keys and reach in and use their mailbox. Thankfully this is a standard and not something that is just left up to whoever is designing the building and the systems. The lower reach limit is bound by the OSHA policies for the post

> *office worker delivering the mail. From an architect's perspective, the room can end up being massive to accommodate each room's mailbox. The benefit is that we don't accidentally cause undue stress or inoperability.*

This may not affect your game, but these types of things are perceivable by the audience, whether they draw attention or are part of the background. Spatially, single family homes vary dramatically from apartments or condos because of this reason. Retrofit solutions also tell stories. A different expectation for a space or occupant than was observed at the point of building.

> Up *uses accessibility to visualize the small ways the couple grows old over time—showing the characters climbing a hill quickly then slowly. Carl takes an old retrofit chairlift up the steep stairs and grumbles at it. In order to make the impacts of age more relatable to young audiences and demonstrate the passage of time, Disney uses the environment to visualize this in addition to the character themselves. This alleviates the requirement for dialogue to say "I am tired" or "this is harder than it used to be." and creates a series of relatable moments.*

Regulations improve predictability and safety. Understanding pertinent codes from a cursory level can provide useful leads for where to deviate. Consistency and generally agreed upon constants also reduce authorship, freeing up creative development for large moves and intentional departures. Again, humans are incredibly susceptible to being primed. Tables, cabinets, lights, doors, and panels are all tied to human reach dimensions for instance. Architects typically do not prioritize their websites and images to respond to searches like "atrium dimensions" or "size of an average hallway." At time of writing, searching certain questions will lead to answers that refer primarily to single family homes. In order to start to break down the mystique of "rules of thumb" here are a few standards I can relay from my experience as someone who has spent a few years working on a variety of projects. My disclaimer here: do not build a literal building using this as a reference.

Gridlines

Gridlines for architects occur at the scale of structure. They are not necessarily square and often do not subdivide the building evenly. One of the most important factors is developing a mental map of the project. Organizing biases or influences on regions as well as developing systems work in a variety of circumstances. Designing a building is certainly not a linear or formulaic procedure. The permitting, coordinating, and safety aspects can be difficult but have a resolution, designing is much more circuitous. In game environments, grids have the role of preventing gaps in the build. This encourages much smaller grids.

One way to start on the right foot is developing a grid that falls into your unit system (IE divisible by 5 if decimal, 4 if fractional). Whether the project has a sole designer or has delegated design to multiple people, this is a tool for maintaining datums. Setting up a grid can help things "fall into place" and allow everyone to be mindful of the priorities. Gridlines can become a framework for teams to contribute without creating problematic conditions. This gives every person contributing to the project a trustworthy point to build off of. These lines define where the builable limits of the site are, structural limitations are, and important visual datums. "Datums" are linear of planar relationships curated during design.

These relationships can establish hierarchy. Gridlines can also give more control to designers looking to use scale to build relationships between spaces. Gridlines can help communicate constraints to a team without hindering creativity. They can provide a quick visual understanding of layout and anticipated spatial needs. This demonstrates expected density of features as well.

Units

Units in built architecture are the basis of communication between trades. It is the means through which architects ensure permitting, fabrication, and inspection. The built environment has two choices, imperial and metric. If being built on site, this decision is made by the location of the building. If it is modular, the decision can be made by the fabricators. Whichever system the building is built in, it must be designed for. In virtual architecture, units are non-universal. This suits the engine and scale of the environment.

As architects are required to provide spaces that are navigable by all humans, one could start to discern the patterns that are, from a design standpoint, "givens." We assume a few things about people. For instance, if 5′ 9″, 1.8 m, is the average height for a male human, we provide a minimum of 6′ 8″, 2.1 m, for head height.

Architects use imperial (ft/in) and metric (m) and must prefer one or the other even if both are indicated. For instance, if we provided a door of 36″ × 80″ or 914 mm × 2032 mm. Notably, both imperial numbers are divisible by 8.

Many building materials work in 4s 8s and 16s, this biases "standard sizes." Alternatively, metric dimensions may look more like 900 mm × 2100 mm or 35.433″ × 82.67″. Metric dimensions can be divisible by modules of 5 or 10. If the design team cannot work with fractions and remainders they must use decimal inches. The fractional relationship of imperial breaks down when using decimal inches as repeating decimals are prevalent.

> *For instance, the module for many imperial designed buildings rely on 4 and 8. There are 12 inches in a foot, inches are subdivided into sixteenths. $4 \times 2 = 8$, $4 \times 3 = 12$, $4 \times 4 = 16$. This is wonderful for fractional relationships as long as systems can consider fractions. A dimension such as 4′ 4″ translates to 4.33333′ or 52″. If decimal foot is chosen, the number cannot be manually typed without risking a gap. If inch is chosen, numbers add up quickly and are in base of 12 if required to go between feet and inches. Without the software's assistance to hold fractions and remainders when locating items, this can become unnecessarily cumbersome.*

In either case, imperial or metric, the more granular of their respective measurements are used to communicate interior dimensions. Exterior dimensions are communicated in feet or meters. Surveys use only decimal units, even when working with feet. This is a factor of increased precision given the tools used. Surveyors use decimal feet for documentation not design, however.

Architects describe dimensions as small as 1/8th of an inch to be considerate of construction tolerances. In reality it is drafted at an accuracy of 1/256th of an inch. This would otherwise require interpretation to determine where to locate a cut or fastener. As these are not considerations in virtual spaces, decimal feet/inches could work with the only complication being introduced by decimals for 4″ and 8″ or ¼″ and ⅛″.

The literal numbers are not as important as ratios, however. Buildings are created for human scale, your projects may need to be larger or smaller to accommodate unique characters' range of motion.

Valve references 3 different units of measure for Half-Life *architecture. "Units" are the equivalent of 16 × the dimension in feet (presumably due to the fact that inches fractionally break down to 1/16ths)—then a conversion from imperial to metric. With the exception of a typo, indicated by the conversion, the dimensions more or less match typical post-ADA American architecture. 8′ ceiling height, 4′ corridor, an inch taller than the minimum 6′ 8″ head height (presumably to the benefit of using 108 instead of 106.666667), and 3′ wide thresholds. I would argue that this redundancy may be a bit much. Using mm as a primary unit could prove to be the most versatile. This would allow fewer spatially imperceptible conversion discrepancies.*

```
Architecture
128 = 8′ 0″ = 2.44 m normal corridor height
64 = 4′ 0″ = 1.22 m normal corridor width
108 = 6′ 9″ = 2.05 m normal door height
48 = 3′ 6″ = 914.4 mm normal door width
```

Modern architects design for a bipedal human, moving at 2–3 mph, 5′ 8″ tall when standing with a reach range of 2′ 6″, provided from a seated or standing position as determined by task. Americans have worked hard to enforce universal design, emphasizing that any built environment should provide an equal experience for all people experiencing it. Your levels will achieve these accessibilities in different ways as you design for metrics like difficulty and time to complete. You are also designing your environment for playable characters, the demographic is has known motion limitations.

Typical Dimensions

Architects are responsible for creating spaces that are safe for humans to build and inhabit. We rely on a variety of sources to ensure this; typically the most stringent are outlined in the Americans Disabilities Act and prescribed by the International Building Code. Graphic Standards provide reference for this as well, but performs more as a resource, derivative of existing codes, for architects rather than a binding code.

For your convenience the following are some rules of thumb that typically make their way into every project. These are calibrated for the expectation that humans are 70″–75″ tall (1905–1790 mm) and 20″–18″ wide (495–450 mm). These also anticipate travel at the pace of walking.

Typical Dimensions		
Reference	Imperial	Metric
Human Height	70" - 75"	1790 mm - 1905 mm
Human Width	18" - 20"	450 mm - 495 mm
Circulation	Imperial	Metric
Ceiling Height	96" - 108"	2440 mm - 2745 mm
Door Opening	80" - 84"	2030 mm - 2130 mm
Guardrail Height (Fall Protection)	42"	1065 mm
Handrail Height	36"	915 mm
Doorknob Height	36"	915 mm
Corridor Width	42" - 54"	1065 mm - 1370 mm
Circulation between furniture	24"	610 mm
Stairs		
Width	36" - 44"	915 mm - 1120 mm
Riser	7"	180 mm
Tread	11"	285 mm
Wheelchair Turn	60" Dia.	1525 mm Dia.
Surfaces	Imperial	Metric
Counter Height	42"	1065 mm
Work Table Desk	29"	735 mm
Low Table	25"	635 mm
Bed	18"	455 mm
Work Chair	17.5"	445 mm

Mobility is unique to games individually, a study of game environments as reference would be amiss without studying the character mobility as well. Providing room for camera may have additional "apparatus" to host camera—forcing dimensions to be taller. As local constraints come into play, these rules of thumb will inevitably be deviated away from. Understanding what makes the space atypical can help designers understand how to detail. In a taller than normal hallway, flooring may be referenced as typical but the wall coverings may have to pull inspiration from taller spaces. Creatively resolving these discrepancies will often lead to a much more interesting solution than forcing a design into a new context with minimal change.

9

Materials

Often materiality of a built structure has some utility. Choosing a material affects the visual, longevity, and construction detailing of a design. The material palette can be determined by time, technology, geopolitical climate, and infrastructure. For this reason we can start to group architecture by region and time period. Styles can emerge when multiple architects come to a similar conclusion, this can be driven by constructability or budget. Materiality, in that sense, can be used as a binding mechanism for cultures or neighborhoods. The logic behind material selection mostly revolves around constructibility. Properties of the materials inform decisions.

Over time, good solutions to familiar problems provide a visual pattern for environments. This perpetuates a regional style, also referred to as a vernacular. While the lay person may not be concerned with a material's function or properties, they can still pick up on the visual of it. Over time, the fabric of the area will exhibit patterns and develop a visual identity. Similar to the way certain cities can stand in for each other when filming, as long as they have similar climates. Climate has a major impact on building exteriors. Interiors are more subject to trends. They often demonstrate the decade of a building as they are less resilient materials and easier to replace with a remodel.

In the built environment materiality changes the means and methods of construction. There are roles and reasons to use each material. For the purpose of designing virtual spaces, we'll skip over specifics on substrates, materials between the faces of a wall. Exterior materials are often selected for their utility as well as their look. Exterior materials are responsible for weather resistance and insulation. Interior materials are often selected for their appearance, as they are veneers or composite materials. Interior materials primarily must not support the spread of fire and transmittance of sound.

As previously mentioned, the whole building does not need to be as resilient as the portion that hits the ground. This nuance not only provides relief from relentless walls of texture. It can also suppose the concept of being resourceful with materials and budget. Changing color, texture, or providing some ornamentation can draw attention as well as break up the monotony. As a result, there are typologies which go hand in hand with the material cladding them. Stone is resilient and lends itself well to monolithic buildings. It is expensive to move as it is a large building material, allowing the owner to demonstrate wealth. It also has gotten a second life as a cladding material when steel was invented. This allowed stone to work as a much thinner building material and become more accessible. Its previous function of covering large surfaces could be made more adaptable.

Materials can be responsible for telling stories, similar to the way word choice can evoke precise parallels in writing. Knowing how materials age and what details can change that or subvert it may be helpful to distinguish something that's meant to be clever from something that was pulled together out of necessity.

Louis Kahn famously remarks on the importance of pondering what the brick "wants to be." This is quite honestly the best way that a concept makes it from early design phases to construction, despite working with different team members and facing cost cutting decisions. We also leverage this "path of least resistance" method for pitching ideas to city design reviews, starting by exploring or contemplating the most operations driven design first.

Architects let the materials' construction properties drive the design as opposed to wrangling it into something it isn't suited to do. For instance, finding places to put columns, aligning courses (rows) of bricks with openings, and creating opportunities for drainage. This causes a host of chain reactions in biases, representation, and literature. To a similar end, architects primarily work orthographically and as a result. An equivalent would be a pilot using only the instruments when weather conditions make external visuals unreliable. Architects have just recently been truly able to work in perspective alongside of orthographic. Functionally, we now have the safety net our theory was trying to create using rules of thumb and numbers. Practically, architects benefit from the logic of associating compositions with numbers because of those seams. Relying on modules that easily break into common denominators can start to create a system, sets the design up for success, reduces waste, and often reduces scrutiny from associated trades.

Virtual architecture is again different as the representation is the final product. There are no additional steps to realization. An architect must cleverly detail materials to make a light material looking heavy. Virtual architecture has far less baggage when iterating through materials. The designer then has authorship over whether or not the building was meant to be constructed. From there questions like "who" constructed this and "when" can start to color design choices. Creating unbuildable details can also open doors. Floating shingles or massive marble halls are jarring and exciting for occupants.

One of the major turning points in the history of building materials is the industrial revolution. This led to the casual use of metal as a building material. As a result, literally every material available has changed. Metal fasteners and reinforcements allow for lighter weight, more minimal details. This sparked a fascination that architects cannot shake—optimizing for minimalism. Developers also perpetuate this as it often costs less as the style has become more popular. The following chapters will explain materials and their properties. They will also take time to depict "before" and "after" being augmented by metal.

Wood

Wood can be used to symbolize a "knowable" construction. It is simple and honest as it works logically. Wood is one of the easiest materials to manipulate. It requires that the civilization has tools and the capacity to cut and saw wood. This gives it a long lineage of precedents from a variety of locations, climates, and cultures. Wood can be cut on site with handheld tools. This puts some capability in the hands of the builder to match the intent rather than relying solely on the drawings provided by the architect. Being able to cut this material on-site, fasten it with screws or nails with limited preparation of holes or penetrations through the material all contribute to its modern prevalence. It is primarily considered as a combustible structural material. For this reason, lightweight wood construction has limits related to height and exposure. Heavy timber has fire resistant properties and as a result can be a visual element of the space as shown below.

Wood has some unique properties related to the fact that it is organic. Unaltered, there is directionality to the strength of wood. With the help of adhesives, plywood and oriented strand board (OSB) spread forces over a surface area. It is typically strongest when forces flow along the grain. Cutting wood into an arc shape simply won't have the same structural properties as bent or faceted wood. This means that joints that require the removal of material compromise the structural integrity of the member. Metal fasteners (screws, nails, anchor bolts) afford less material to lose when connecting framing members. It also afforded the transition from a solely structural material to an affordable cladding material.

Modern wood construction leverages the predictability available through modern sawing procedures as shown below.

Wood, of course, is an organic material with flaws and deformation. It's also quite vulnerable to water and insects. These considerations discourage extended contact with the ground. As a result, stone or concrete are at the base of buildings fairly frequently. Reducing flat wood surfaces, understanding that decks allow some sort of drainage below is another high priority. Modern wooden walls consist of studs and plates as shown below.

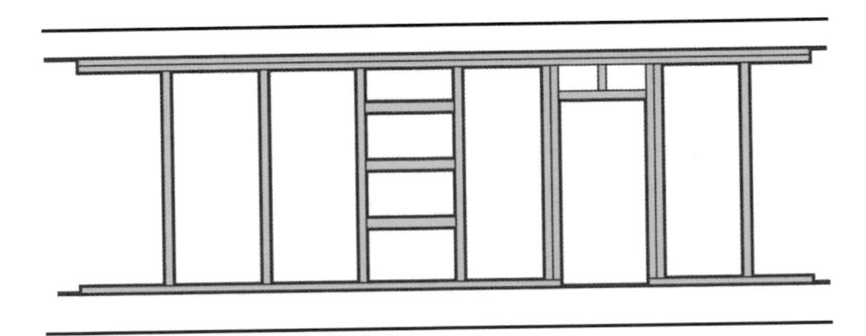

They are typically clad with plywood and gypsum board. The base plate provides a nailer for the studs. A standard wood frame construction is 2×6 studs spaced 12″–18″ apart with some studs bundled together into columns. Then they're tied together with a double top plate to help spread out weight across the entire wall. Easy for two people to assemble and modify on site.

Metal strips and nails are used to keep wood in the right place to transfer structural loads. Any of these pieces falling out of plane could compromise the flow of force to the bearing soil.

Wood structures will typically be lighter weight to reduce cost. If fire resistance is required, there are treated lumbers available or a larger section of lumber. Both create a char layer on the outside of the necessary section of lumber for carrying the load. It can perform predictably for hours to maintain the integrity of the building in a fire event.

Wood is also easy to turn into elaborate shapes. Handheld power tools can accurately cut wood with minimal training. Turning and milling have a somewhat low bar for entry unlike manipulating steel. As a result, it's pretty common to see interior stair balusters and moulding adorned in intricate wood details as shown below.

Designing in wood typically starts with the end result, figure a way to get in the general vicinity of what you'd like it to look like. A key design feature is the Lincoln logs approach, since materials usually do not perfectly intersect but instead prefer to bear on flat surfaces. Most joints leverage this in conjunction with gravity as shown below.

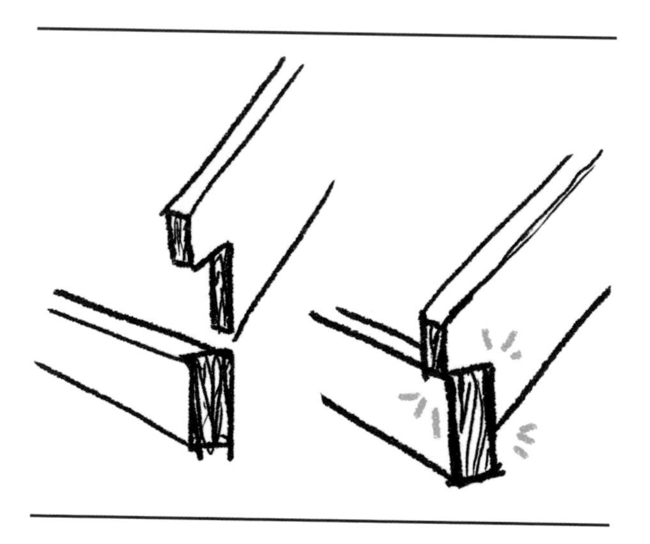

Joints are strongest when the weight of the structure increases friction which reduces the risk of failure. Surprisingly enough, wood works pretty much the same at the balsa wood scale that the glue is nails or nail plates. Relying solely on the nails to keep a joint together is typically not the best idea. More often than not, nails work best when they're keeping something in place laterally and the flow of forces aren't running perpendicular to nails. They primarily assist with shear forces through nail plates, an array of nails. They perform best fastening against shearing movement. Screws of course have a bit more capacity to secure less straightforward joints.

Most wood used as cladding is not load-bearing, which grants the material more freedom. Wood can be nailed directly to a surface as cladding. It can also be held off from the surface to create a rain screen. Stacking and layering are how wood is most typically used. It needs help from metal fasteners to make perfect corners where the horizontal pieces can terminate into a vertical piece. Wood siding is a residential material that is easily manipulated. The thin slats are easy to assemble and are small enough to diminish any imperfections. The striped pattern they create can vary in scale and orientation. The primary goal of this material is to avoid having water getting through the grooves and into the wall. The profile contains a drip edge and a gap large enough to not allow cohesion to draw water into the assembly. The seams can be planned such that they line up with sills and headers, if not wood trim can surround the opening. The introduction of a new system breaks the expectation that the window should interact with that field.

Concrete

Concrete is one of the strongest modern materials. Unlike wood, it is only malleable during design stages. It requires planning and precision to be used in large quantities. Cement is the term for uncured concrete. Cement is a slurry that consists of sand, water, and lime. It can be transported in its separate parts, mixed, and cured on site. "Forms" or boards are coated in oil and used to shape cement as it cures to concrete. After curing, the forms can be released. Ideally, it is also homogenous, which means forces will flow through it like a bridge. Modern concrete is typically poured into forms around steel reinforcing bars. It takes about 28 days for it to cure to its ultimate strength.

Historically, it is an old material, perpetuated by its ease of movement to a site and its durability. Concrete was first used as flooring in 6500 BC. The modern mixture for cement, using portland cement, was introduced in 1824. By 1880 we see the first use of rebar to "prevent walls from spreading."

Cement is mixed on-site by the contractor, its quality is dependent on a skilled and organized construction team. Concrete shares a lot of its properties between vertical and horizontal applications. The horizontal applications have opportunities for thinner slabs and can leverage tensioned cables with a thinner profile than rebar. A faster, more predictable material would be to use Concrete Masonry Units (cinder blocks). These are created offsite and are a bit more forgiving in poor site conditions or for later removal. Once cured, concrete and CMU are both fire and water resistant. Forces work primarily in compression. The exception to this is shell structures leverage smooth curvature to distribute forces outward and down. Concrete is a great candidate for the structure of buildings, even if clad in other materials. Ad-mixtures can be introduced to concrete to customize the way it cures, colors, and strength.

After steel was invented, it was embedded in concrete in a variety of ways in order to give tensile strength to concrete. Even though it has a ton of compressive strength after chemically curing, concrete can only do so well without some tougher material working in tension. The expansion and contraction rates of both materials are close enough to pour cement around reinforcing bars. Rebar is formed into a cage or a grid and provides flexibility to an otherwise stiff material. Longer spans can warrant the use of cables in sleeves to allow an even greater span length. For instance, floor slabs resist "punching" at columns and sag at the midpoint between two supports. Steel offers a way to even out forces without changing the shape of the concrete.

Visually, concrete has a variety of finishes. While its strength and permanence persists, it can look warm, protective, and solemn just using the finish. That's not even considering the effects of aging. By design, texture, or finish of the material lends itself to the function of the surface. Planters can look approachable when stamped with textures. A smaller articulation with wood grain impressed in the surface breaks down the scale of an otherwise massive surface. Form ties break the concrete down into grids.

> *Frank Lloyd Wright's Millard House is a rare Mayan Revival style house. It uses concrete with coffering on wall and ceiling surfaces. This provides a visual tie between the vertical and horizontal surfaces, mirroring the similarity of their utility.*

Structurally, concrete has many applications, most notably its resistance to fire. It is a resilient and durable floor. As a vertical assembly, or wall, concrete is incredibly strong against shear forces. Most modern applications are cast in place, meaning that the depth of the wall can vary by inches instead of modules. The challenges associated with it come from modern technology and codes. Tendons can be post-tensioned and will snap the entire floor if one is accidentally severed. Penetrations must be fire stopped, creating an opening in the wrong place, then placing another adjacent creates a condition that cannot be firestopped with ring-shaped hardware and requires another. Certainly solutions exist to develop on-site design solutions and retrofits, but they just carry some minor barriers that make this material less enticing than wood for smaller structures.

Zaha's CAC demonstrates the different textures of concrete as they perform a variety of functions. Hadid ushers the public in by continuing the concrete from the sidewalk into the building and up the wall. This gesture also allows the concrete to characterize itself through texture. It's scored and rough at the sidewalk, honed in the lobby, and has a formwork texture as it turns into a wall. By breaking out the finishes as a unique trait associated with function, she differentiates an otherwise seamless union of the material.

Scarpa's Brion cemetery uses concrete to create a permanent geometric integration into landscape. His use of geometric shapes and continuity pay homage to ritualistic imagery. Intertwined large- and small-scale articulations allow a variety of readings to emerge—again, blending the responsibility of vertical and horizontal surfaces. Planes of colors can gain depth and variety through minor articulations—this could lead to a variety of interpretations. This of course is the observer projecting their own experiences on an abstract canvas. Floating a rectangular prism above a reflecting pond above a path can symbolize an antithesis of lowering a casket into the ground. Introducing "lines" to a 3d space can hold symbolic value or simply define masses. Lines can accent material, outlining, bisecting, hiding, shining can symbolize the passing of time, or a pathway or winding road. Its symmetry forces it into another world, which could mean the duality of the location—being transported to a closer location to your loved ones, being a monument to their memories and distinctly not belonging to the observer but the observed.

Masonry

As previously mentioned, using materials that are easy to get on-site is important. Masonry describes individual units of material and assembled on site. This includes anything from stone to bricks to terra cotta to glass block. The craftsmanship that goes into creating a wall through the assembly of pieces facilitates opportunities for patterns and ornamentation without a significant addition to the cost of the cladding or labor. The modular nature of masonry allows it to stay current with modern trends as it is customizable in pattern, color, shape, and texture.

Prior to the industrial revolution, masonry walls were unreinforced and brittle. Brick walls were typically made of multiple layers of brick as shown below.

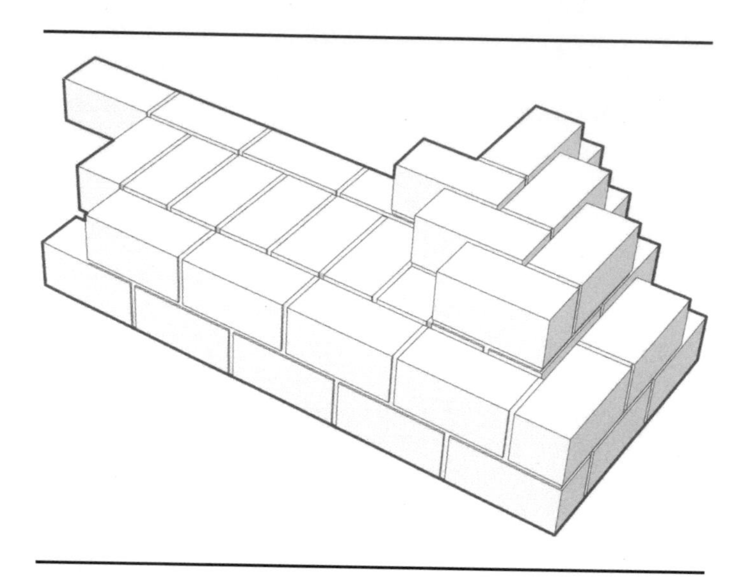

Bricks used in tandem with metal ties are able to create a cavity wall which can be filled with grout as shown below.

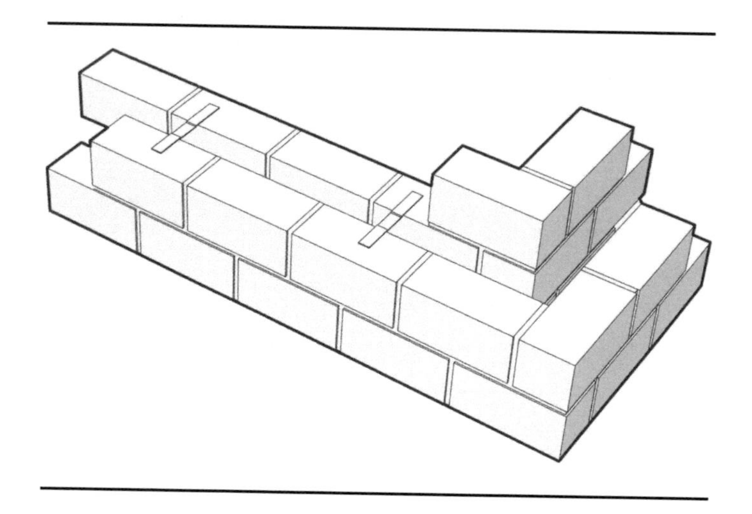

The most typical application of modern brick is a veneer clipped to a backup wall as shown below. This allows the load bearing portion of the wall to keep its structural integrity in a seismic event.

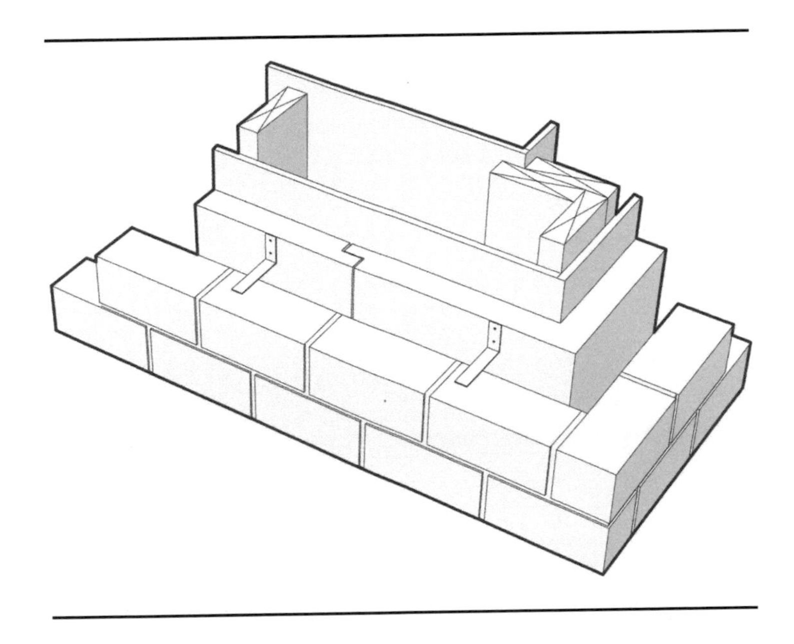

Stone often clads public buildings, symbolizing stability and permanence. Modern applications see it applied as a thin veneer, which can be clipped to a backup wall. Stone accents on sills and lintels are used for their resilience and appearance.

Bricks offer a wide variety of colors and patterns as well as applications. In general, bricks are about the size of a hand. Modular bricks are 3-5/8″ (depth) × 2-1/4″ (height) × 7-5/8″ (length) and are typically brought to their nominal dimensions with 3/8″ mortar joints (approximately 100 mm × 50 mm × 200 mm). As previously mentioned, brick patterning affords the customization of this material to have site specific significance. Some of the most common patterns are common bond, English bond, Flemish bond, running bond, and stacked bond as shown Figures 9.1–9.5, respectively.

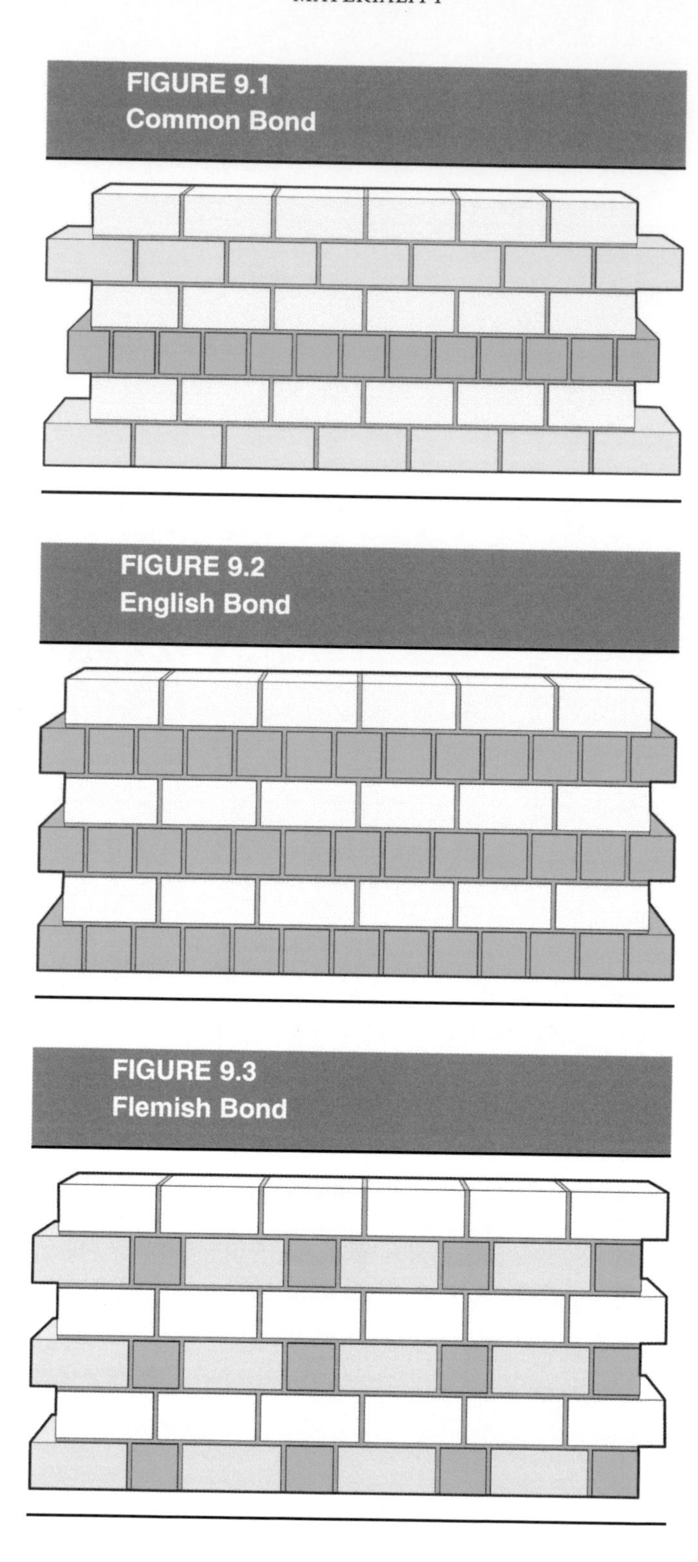

FIGURE 9.1
Common Bond

FIGURE 9.2
English Bond

FIGURE 9.3
Flemish Bond

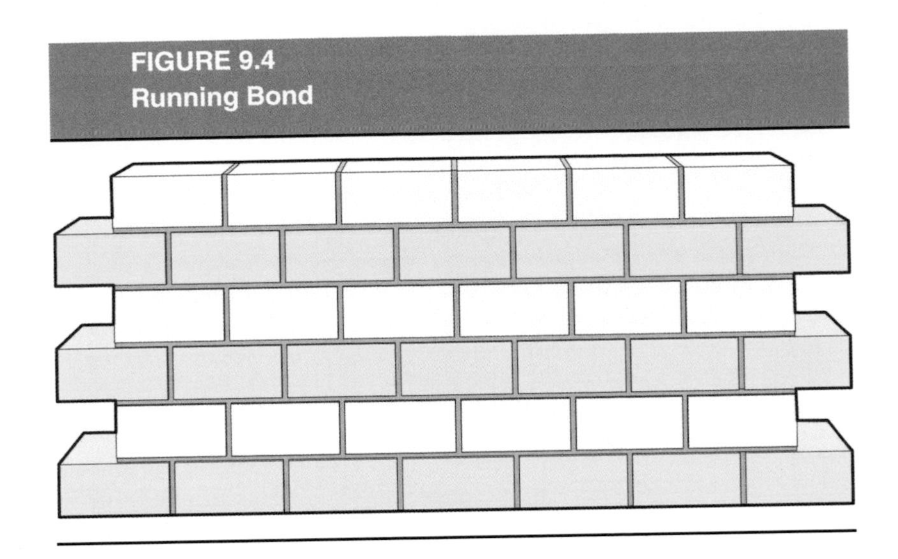

FIGURE 9.4
Running Bond

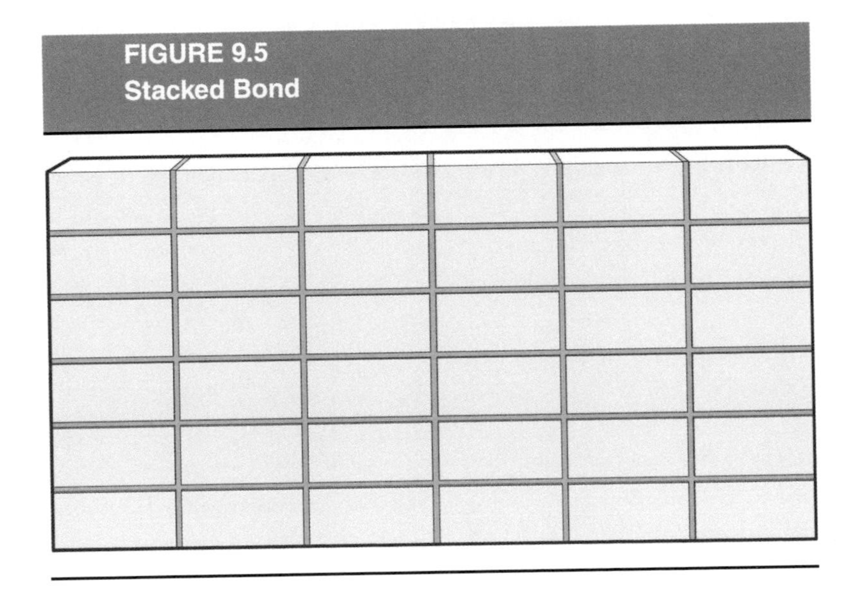

FIGURE 9.5
Stacked Bond

As rooms and buildings scale up to accommodate a wider range of motion, brick sizes can scale up too.

> The Last Of Us *requires extra wide doorways and hallways for maneuvering and combat. As a result, the buildings consist of utility (1 course = 4″) and standard (3 courses = 8″) bricks. They also leverage CMU bricks in utility areas; this is very typical as they are often an inexpensive way to build a fire rated wall. These blocks are 7-5/8″ (depth) × 7-5/8″ (width) × 15-5/8″ (length) and are typically grey. This nuance allows the Boston environment to look rusticated and utilitarian in an incredibly humanist way. Allowing flexibility for materials to tell more specific information about environments allows a variety of interior levels to have personality.*

Window sills and headers can be detailed in bricks by changing their orientation. Many neighborhoods will ask architects to use brick on new buildings to match a certain look or ensure longevity. Bricks can also take on curves and become perforated screens, again with the help of orientation. Because of their scale in comparison to the wall they are creating, there is an opportunity to deviate from a perfectly flat faced wall. This is a blessing and a curse, while maintaining a planar surface is challenging, there are plenty of patterns which break up the monotony of a perfect running bond. The square profile which happens every four courses is a brick rotated 90 degrees to tie together two wythes of brick. We still see this as ornament in veneer or panelized applications. The holdover indicates a preference for the visual appeal despite the vestigial function.

Modern architecture employs a brick veneer with a backup wall. Brick walls fail at grout joints, this leads to a tendency for the entire wall to kick out if not adequately tied back.

Metals

Architecturally, metal can be used as a cladding, structure, and fasteners. Metal panels, cast bronze, wrought iron, shingles, pressed ceiling tiles, and flooring panels are opportunities for planes of material. Structural applications use the material more judiciously, often relying on the minimum profile required, two deep chords to resist deformation and a light web to connect them. Steel framing members come in a variety of different profiles as shown below.

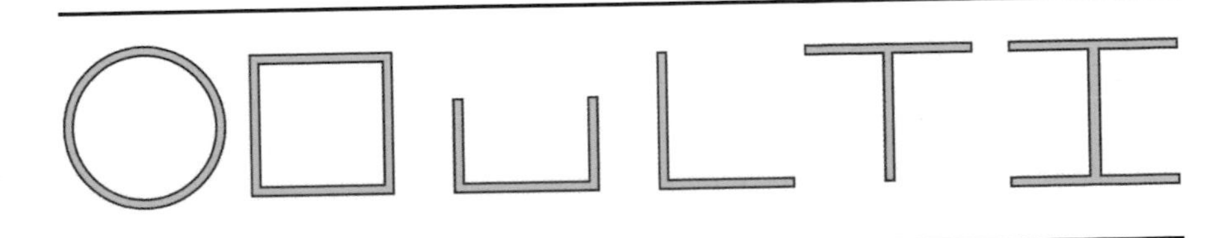

Steel can also be used to augment other materials as shown below, in the case of rebar or post-tensioned cables embedded in concrete to increase spans and reduce cracking.

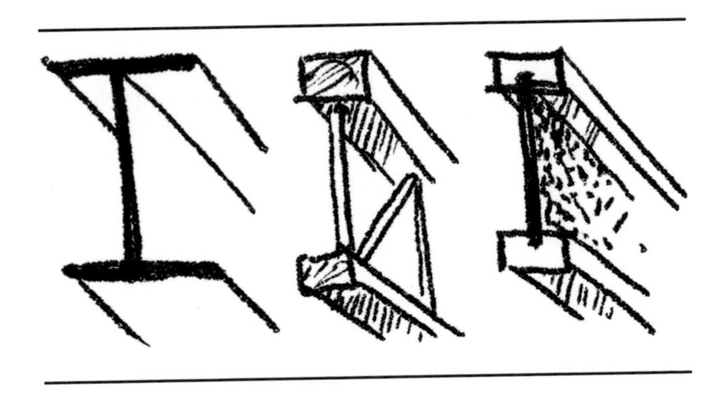

Fasteners refer to screws, nails, masonry ties, and clips all provide lateral bracing to a backup wall, proliferating a wider variety of cladding materials.

Metal as a cladding element has been a long time staple of architecture, as early as 800 AD, bronze has been used to adorn and ornament buildings. In the 1850s, manufacturing technology was able to consistent enough to support architecture structurally using Iron. Closely following was steel in 1885. Our first structural steel building was the Home Insurance Building. It functionally leverages the controlled conditions of a factory to achieve the minimum profile of structure. Wide flanges and angles are incredibly helpful to achieving thinner profiles when supporting forces that are out of plane. So much so that it pushed lightweight wood construction forward with hybrid steel and wood trusses as well as an entirely wood webbed joist.

Joists and beams are typically oriented such that the load is supported in the long direction and shorter flanges are provided to laterally to stabilize the load. Combustible materials that follow this form are more vulnerable to fire than a solid profile. As steel is a noncombustible[1] building material, it simply becomes more efficient through this profile change.

The challenge of working with metal is that it has to be sorted out before it arrives on site. Taking agency out of the construction teams' hands changes how nimble a team can be with design changes on site. Welding also limits construction schedules to avoid damaging glass or certain finishes. There are a variety of attachment methods, most requiring more metal to either weld or fasten columns and beams together. These will typically intersect each other, relying on plates to transfer load between members.

Unfortunately, metal doesn't always play nice with other materials, especially metals. In fact, there's a whole chart of metals that conflict and corrode when in contact with one another. This is a great way to identify the thoughtfulness or planning that went into a detail. Visually, this is indicated by streaks or stains along a surface near fasteners or material changes.

Glass

Glazing is a general term for a variety of glass assemblies. Glass had gone through a few different life cycles. First off, it's expensive to punch a hole in your building's exterior in order to get a translucent face. Forces flow downward and must use a beam to transfer over the nonsupporting area. Most glazing can be characterized by how it's being held in place. Windows are a punch in a wall, supported by the same material as the wall typically. Channel glass and glass block have integral strength and, while some loads need to be diverted, they can function as a wall for the most part.

Curtain wall, window wall, and storefront are distinct from a construction point of view, but as far as virtual architecture goes, most visuals represent something close to "curtain wall." Separated lights refer to a bunch of small pieces of glass that are supported by muntins. Simulated separation refers to a large piece of glass with an applied separator. Certain systems integrate

[1] If exposed, it is still "fireproofed" in most jurisdictions even if in a sprinklered building to extend its elastic range

columns into the system. Curtain wall applications offer unique opportunities to provide corner views. Architects will typically take advantage of this and additionally work to minimize the profile obscuring the corner view as shown below.

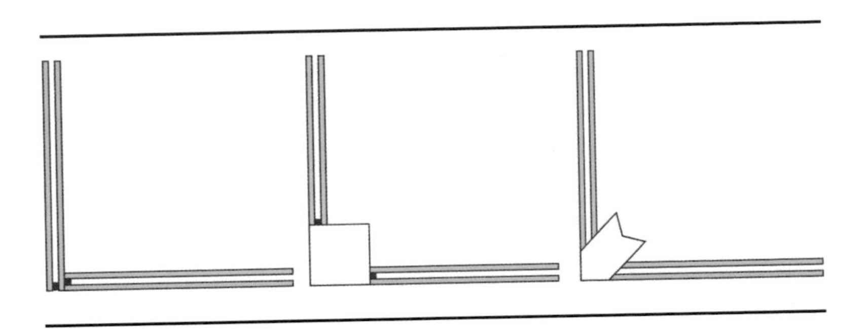

The actual glass is not incredibly expensive as a material. The fact that it cannot be load bearing does have expensive repercussions. A wall is anywhere from 0.9 m to 0.15 m wide. A double-panel glass assembly is 0.025 m. From a structural standpoint, this is an opening in the wall. This means the surrounding structure and wall in the immediate area need to divert forces around it. This creates a unique challenge and importance around creating the space to put glass in a project.

Glass has two primary functions: providing light in and views out. The patterning of windows is often a necessity created by the previous two, connecting the exterior to the interior. In other words, openings are viewed from the exterior as well as interior.

Windows were previously locked between bearing walls, their pattern could only work as long as it fits into the structural bay. Rose windows, stained glass, and architraves articulated design intent with craftsmanship. Architects exhausted varieties of facades shifting windows, pairing them with ornamentation. Searching for opportunities to create rhythm and hierarchy within the constraint of structure was a major design feature. When steel allowed for windows to float freely about the facade, the paradigm shifted. A new variety of viable patterns were thrown into existence. The facade could choose to accentuate the structural organization of the building or tell a completely new story. Modern windows can take responsibility for shaping spaces and sculpting light. This creates a decision point, which had previously existed as a given.

Manufactured Materials

Composite building materials are an affordable and durable cladding solution. These suppliers are incredibly efficient and inexpensive. This market trend affects the bulk of new buildings currently being developed. Materials that can cover massive facades without articulation are now in vogue. Manufactured materials also reduce the amount of decisions related to transitioning materials. Design has gotten "safer" we've seen the emergence of plain manufactured materials. These are unlike traditional materials as they do not have an autological design language. This means that they clad the building with the intent of providing minimal commentary on what they are made of. The implications of subverting this expectation can best be described by starting with what would be missing.

Choosing wood, for instance, depicts the form it wraps as well as a secondary meaning which may indicate warmth or human scale. The grain has an opportunity to provide scale, giving a reference for how large the building is or how close the viewer is to it. It is familiar and measurable. Wood siding is also a familiar building material, allowing some portion of the conversation shift toward collective consciousness. We see Aalto use wood in Villa Maeria in a variety of configurations, expanding the expectation for the material to change forms as its function changes.

There are preconceived ideas about what colors are available, how it can be fastened, what it feels like. Subverting the existing understanding of a material brings a lot of authorship to what form is being created and what material is chosen. It calls into question, what is so pure of a concept that it must be devoid of texture and materiality to convey its idea? Answering that may be Superstudio's Continuous Monument, or Boulee's Cenotaph to Newton.

By creating and cladding a building in a synthetic material that does not depict its own origin, it allows the architecture to be more responsible for the form it takes. In some ways this does honestly depict the construction of the building, as drywall is a required component for any fire rated wall.

Many manufactured materials revolve around cement fiber. The pulp can be formed into reasonably flat, an inexpensive boards with a variety of texture and finish combinations. It is being used primarily for its cost but its personality is benign. The lack of commentary provides varying levels of design commitment.

Manufactured quartz or stone has also gotten a lot of traction recently. Authorship and intentionality gets baked into the false stone face of the material. This allows things such as predictability and higher uniformity. As a result architects are now able to get perfect bookmatching, and patterning over long distances without fault.

As far as the theoretical implications of choosing a minimally articulated palette go, modernism paved the way. Luxury as demonstrated by unblemished materials became more achievable over time. It can also be perceived as a willful boast against recognizable scales and articulation. Providing detailing and patterns help occupants to determine the scale of a building. The "paper model" school of design may have begun as a rebellion but quickly developed a new minimum viable product for developers. Now, paradigms have shifted and the default choice in many market driven buildings leads toward the materials with less articulation.

In the complete other end of the spectrum, synthetic materials are being leveraged for very custom graphics. The 2.5D aspect of an applied material to a 3D surface creates a precise experience. The image applied to the surface becomes a point of critique, as it can be literal or abstract. This is also not a choice architects have the luxury of making for a built structure.

Part IV

Character

One of the most common questions I get from game designers is "How do you give an environment a feeling like (any other place)?" As suggested in previous chapters, building styles are most often a result of similar constraints, either culturally or physically. The most complex solution would be to assume the same constraints. The least complex solution would be to adopt some of the textures created by those constraints. Details and compositions are vehicles for motifs explored by forms and massing. In architectural lore, complex narratives and world views can be communicated through the architect or patron using architecture, finding opportunity to communicate through setting up and redefining expectations. The development of an architectural language is important to creating something that leaves room for interpretation. Achieving this duplicity takes an understanding of potential solutions and landing on one. This offers the viewer some authorship as to what it could mean and why both can or should exist.

Seeing this simply requires a creative interpretation. Creating the canvas that fuels this takes a little extra theory. Supposing that theory has weight is the first step.

One of the most telling stories about architectural theory goes back to the theoretical repercussions of a landscape (horizontal) window. One would imagine this is simply a function of the shape of the room viewing outward or the type of view created. Corbusier and Perret argued over multiple letters about what this meant for the composition of the room, how deep light could reach into the space, how it related to human proportions.

> Corbusier continues the polemic with Perret in an argument in Precisions, demonstrating "scientifically" that the fenêtre en longueur illuminates better, by relying on a photographer's chart that gives times of exposure. Though photography (as with film) is based on single-point perspective, between photography and perspective there is an epistemological break. —'Le Corbusier and Photography' - Beatriz Colomina

Modern architects have the luxury of designing windows that don't relate to plans. Their exchange marks a time where paradigm shifted and a "known" variable went away. The adjustment to this was not insignificant. Modern transitions to new forms relate to digital fabrication. Fabricators can make a variety of different profiles and shapes, software with the capacity to accurately convey complex geometries have made this process more accessible. In curvilinear and parametric architecture, "apertures" or non-rectilinear windows are more related to the exterior than interior in many cases. Most buildings remain rectilinear, but certainly have benefitted from these advancements none the less.

10

Detailing

One aspect that severely separates architecture from all other mediums is assembly—the means through which the project comes together from discrete pieces. Architecture relies on an organization between the major structure and its individual elements. This means supposing architecture as a machine with pieces that come together into a sum greater than its parts.

In order to appear cohesive, monumental, or heroic, diminishing the role of individual pieces is important. The opposite—thoughtful, tailored, and cozy requires an incredible amount of detail paid to make each piece seem like it has a role to play.

In absence of construction constraints, justification becomes more situational. Over thousands of years of material research and applications, architecture has developed textures unique to materials and locations. These textures manifest through detailing and the infinitely many decisions that must be made in order to fabricate a building. As previously mentioned, answering all of these constraints in a virtual environment will become unnecessarily burdensome. Artistic license is incredibly important to determining how to leverage these textures in the most productive way for a team. Design manuals can provide some consideration toward making decisions about this. Providing consistent direction on believability and level of detail is important to the execution an immersive environment.

Developing virtual designs with thoughtful details implies that some limits occur in the world. Aligning this with fiction and lore that already exists in the world can contribute to a more immersive world. At first glance, this may not seem necessary for virtual architecture (not assembled by tangible elements) but is simply an additional canvas for characterizing the environment.

Occupants may register this information below the level of consciousness, but still be able to tell whether or not the location was cohesive, seemed expensive, or inexpensive. Small features which may have originally been introduced to cover up challenging details have made their way into what most people expect a room to have, like trim over corners. Large features which cover material transitions, like a flat roof masonry building with a cornice, articulate and terminate the facade.

This chapter will shed some light on construction techniques and their visual impact on design. The replication of these details will not serve as a basis of good design. The point of this chapter is to give designers confidence running down a new path. As luck would have it, architects and developers are still in love with modern or minimalist principles. Undoubtedly, it is easier to design and, with modern materials, fabricate details that focus on diminishing their appearance. Reveals between panels is more common than seams. Fastener locations are not often celebrated on cladding materials.

Some deciphering may be required to bring the subtleties to light again as the gap between historical architecture and current architecture seems wildly different. In many cases, we're seeing buildings that supply a more airtight, sophisticated, or compact solution to an age old problem. We'll look at problem areas and try to understand how different time periods and different materials have informed the decision.

Seams

A somewhat challenging portion of architecture to learn is "composition." Generally, composition is depicted by pieces coming together; however, designing with that vision from the start is challenging. In practice, the building is first visualized as its maximum extents before articulation occurs. This changes the development of the building's composition from being an additive process to creating and adjusting seams. Under built conditions, limits of materials contribute primarily to the location of seams. Often complexity and ornamentation falls into an order on the facade. Historically ornamentation delineated seams and limits, like icing on a gingerbread house. A difficult seam, such as a header for a window or a rooftop is afforded extra decoration. Architects generally prefer an opportunity to characterize the facade over trying to blend dissimilar edges. Cornices are a great example of this, leveraging dentils to diminish the visual impact of a wavering profile across the length of a building. A broader profile hides the parapet top which can look flimsy from grade and gives a more pleasing appearance that is easier to control. In contrast, details can be arrayed over a whole facade to make a field condition. Metal clips, mullions, or panels can work together to create a condition along a facade additionally to their role structurally.

Seams could be as simple like a row of windows with a door in the mix. Often, the heads will line up. If the windows need to reach higher than the door, a muntin or mullion should be introduced to hold the line of the door through the window. It can also help designers transition from more stringent structural constraints to more open floor plans as loads decrease on upper floors. In order to achieve flat hierarchy, or uniformity, the most stringent requirement becomes the "typical" condition. For instance, if one floor needs a taller clearance designers may need to change the articulation of the floor if it affects the design of the facade. Virtual architecture does not require interior and exterior unity, meaning that there is authorship tied to this decision as well. Virtual architecture opts in to the complexity that built structures must address in order to be occupiable.

Demonstrating public versus private spaces often happens in buildings as a side effect of value engineering. Higher quality finishes will be focused in areas of higher visibility. The lowest visibility spaces, mechanical or maintenance spaces, will have a more utilitarian look to them. Being clever about how money has been rationed out

> *In the animated movie* Spirited Away, *we see precise detail and accuracy shown for vignettes and portions of the building, but the artists were clever to focus their efforts. The level of detail for the facade changes as you move from public to service spaces. Public spaces are highly ornamented wood work to plain stucco with punched openings. This works with the narrative and still holds intentionality though visually depicting a variety of styles and detailing choices. This show of restraint and attention to detail gives the background agency to affect the perception of the scene beyond simply demonstrating the location of the characters at a point in time.*

This is precisely the challenge that many municipalities tackle using design guidelines. They direct a variety of contributors (architects) to create buildings with individuality that work with the existing context. To create a system that isn't charged with delaying schedules, the city often opts to define what makes a "good space." Often, this is an imperfect system as it relies on symptoms of good design to create rules. City planners are looking to repeat the success of existing buildings. Municipal codes coined the term "secondary architectural elements" to help provide a rubric for new architecture to meet a certain standard of facade details. Requiring a variety of materials as, if left unrestricted, could easily turn into a monolithic and overwhelming face of a building. Subdivided surfaces also make aging less apparent, providing neighborhood less reliant on maintenance.

Functionally, materials have different strengths and weaknesses. Changing materials based on interior function, visibility outward, or views of the building itself, are all reasonable decision points to consider. As previously mentioned, this can entirely be subverted by building the environment as individual sets. Virtual architecture cannot rely on "necessity" to demand material change. It does, however, contribute to the nuance and storytelling potential for a design. Finding reasons to introduce bay windows, for instance, may contribute to the profile or "residential" look of a building. Of course, there is no bias which forces the hand of the artist to look for an opportunity. For virtual architecture, the rules and rationales for breaking up the facade would become self-inflicted. Arguments defined through function, cost-effectiveness, or believability would then be filtered through the lens of narrative.

Material transitions are often an indicator of sophistication or thoughtfulness. When two materials meet, they may need to observe different rules near and edge condition. In fact, most details drawn for a building's construction set will pertain to edge conditions. One very important one is flooring as it approaches a wall. Hospitals will actually use curved transitions in certain rooms to make them easier to clean. Stone flooring may change pattern near walls to reduce the number of cuts in the material. One of the only flooring materials that boldly charges through all vertical obstacles is concrete. As demonstrated in most renderings, tools to do this are somewhat challenging to keep track of through design changes. In fact, we often represent it symbolically or with words in schedules and specifications.

Material changes don't necessarily have to happen at walls and columns, changing materials can be great for dividing spaces without walls. It can indicate completion of a thought or an invitation to keep exploring an area. Material changes in flooring are often related to material changes on the ceiling. The two horizontal assemblies find similar patterns available as they are affected by the walls enclosing the space. A common trend is to simply announce when a space is a corridor, indicating linear movement, and when a space is a room, indicated by a border.

Characterization

Understanding how these constraints impact styles in the built environment can help continuity of stories in a fictional world. Much like cooking, the ingredients are one part of the recipe. If you were to design two neighborhoods within a city, showing a relationship using the material palette could be useful, but not bind them to the same character. For instance, one could be where working people live, simple but sturdy details would convey that. In contrast, fussy details with complex interactions of materials could indicate a more aristocratic street. These nuances naturally occur in the built environment, often demarcated with more elaborate street furniture and planting as well.

> *The City of Seattle uses light poles to visually characterize neighborhoods. Certain parts of the city will have wooden poles, these are the most cost efficient. A step-up frame there is—the metal poles with a square base and chamfered edges. These are not particularly decorative but are resilient and have efficient-looking luminaires. The most ornate light post is the Chief Seattle base with ornamental spherical luminaires. Seattle City Light has a system for when and where bases and luminaires should be used. Most of the locations which have upgraded lightpole also support other tourism infrastructure, like maps and additional street name signage. These serve as wayfinding tools for tourists looking for directions and activities.*

The planning required to influence the look of a city and taxes required to carry out that plan will not uniformly transform a city. A variety of zones and upgrade cycles also limit how sweeping these changes can realistically be. This conflict has an opportunity to support themes inequality or subverted to make an uncanny utopia. Whether acknowledged or not, this will impact the perception of the player. These details will help you provide visual support to the story, and potentially help the player generate original thoughts as a reaction to the space in its context.

This divergence dramatically changes the opportunities and priorities between the two industries. As a result, I focus on the rationale behind the thesis as opposed to the details as they will need to be tailored to individual conditions. Even if the style of a game is realistic in rendering, the gameplay forces adaptation of any built structure.

Fallout games are based on real-life cities, the quests and desired gameplay experience force abstraction. As a result, buildings may be posed like movie sets to get a desired look.

This is part of the challenge of creating a game rather than a movie, losing agency of the camera. By giving up the camera angles, the world must act as an entertainer or director to the player. As a result of this, there are some clever tricks that may not render an accurate depiction of a building but would render a great environment. For that reason, I will suggest these rules of thumb as a springboard, keeping in mind a great amount of curation is required additionally to create a successful environment.

Plenty of games leverage this material accurately, my favorite is *Breath of the Wild*. They have two separate applications which help identify a key difference between two of the villages in the game. It also codifies the characteristics of the civilizations that built them.

The Rito Village is what we would consider lightweight wood frame construction as shown below.

Fabric is used as a cladding material, which is uniquely advantaged in virtual architecture. Ritos, like birds, can fly so wind direction is important, so feathers and fabric could feasibly serve a purpose. This also allows a visual correlation to fuselages and gliders. Establishing this demonstrates contrast to the goron village's heavy timber construction. This works twofold as the Gorons have large hands and most likely would not care to articulate handrails with fine details as shown below.

So there's a lot of ways the level characterizes itself, but it also manages to foreshadow events as well. Like directors, the level designers and environment artists decorated these scenes with props. It's exceptionally impressive when these work after giving camera control to the player.

Using the same material to a variety of capacities also helps create a comparison between two dissimilar things. Whether the player actively considers it, wood is a charming and warm material. By creating two distinct looks that play off of this in different ways, the player can be reminded of one when seeing the other.

Often characterization occurs indirectly for architecture. Architecture will often depict the Zeitgeist of the era in which it is created. Inevitably, this occurs because pressures, politics, technologies, and cultures have an amazing impact on the design of architecture. If a material is hard to come by or labor prices skyrocket, architects and owners will react to it. As it is a very slow industry, these changes can take place over enough time to have a few buildings react to the temporary constraints. When the pressures change, trends emerge as a result of a new set of boundaries and "givens." At this point a style is able to be identified, looking back.

> *International style developed as a result of globalism. The fascination of western cultures identifying architecturally with similar constraints sparked a desire to learn from one another. Details and structural designs made available through steel were funded by post-war increased capacity for manufacturing steel. This created a wave of steel and glass buildings, subtle variations affording unique articulation vertically and horizontally. At that time, sophistication and technological advancements could be depicted by using delicate materials together.*

Wang Shu recognized an opportunity to create a regional style and later national style for china by changing formwork on concrete. Instead of working to imitate the look of western concrete work, Shu experimented with bamboo forms. This allows a texture which creates alternate readings as well as gives more information about the culture and context in which these projects exist.

Support

The primary goal of this chapter is to document the types of support that exist in support of their use as a texture or canvas for ornament. Graphical statics is a visual way of organizing the way forces interact with structural elements. Spending time finding how wide the columns would realistically have to be for a certain area may overburden your design. Simply leveraging the logic employed by engineers and architects to distribute load to the ground can create compelling levels. Most caveats in this book allude to it, but it may make the most sense here to explain. Accuracy is not incredibly important compared to narrative.

Two factors create the ambiguity preventing an unbiased numeric answer. First, there are countless design choices in the built environment that are not visually represented. Also a host of data points are required to achieve said accuracy. They are typically designed for a safety factor of six and also consider live loads, dead loads, seismic, and wind loads. Structural members are hierarchically organized to include some redundancy for failure. There are infinitely many portions of the structural calculation that have no visual impact on the spaces created other than depth and makeup of an assembly. Second, gravity in your game may not be 9.8 m/s/s. The designers would then have to choose whether or not the space should look accurate compared to human environments or if it is about exploring the impacts of a different gravity. These things considered, selective accuracy could serve as a great springboard for creating a successful texture or system for spaces you create. There is a middle ground between developing spaces that don't look like they're defying gravity and ones that are overburdened by an immaterial constraint.

Material selection for a structural member can rely on a variety of conditions. Utility often drives material choice in a building, as you may have seen in previous chapters. Built designs will typically track with spatial and monetary limits. Architects are most familiar with spatial constraints but will typically make decisions understanding with a general understanding of cost implications. Each material has different construction functionalities. Generally, wood is inexpensive but labor can add cost with complicated details. Concrete is reasonable even considering the expense of rebar. It gains efficiency when forms can be reused and details are simple. Glass is somewhat expensive due to the extra support needed to divert structural loads around it. Aluminum is expensive and steel is very expensive. Both have a tendency to be fabricated off site and assembled on site, this can afford complicated details to a certain extent. Some patterns emerge from these knowns. Architects customarily use metal as a fastener, accent, or reinforcement material. Timber structures often use metal fasteners, plates, and connections. Steel (rebar) helps reinforce concrete. These material changes require some thought as to which materials are interacting, how they are assembled, and how they will age.

The point of connection between materials is the basis of articulation for many architects. The limitations and biases introduced by steel, embellished by architects founded the Chicago School fundamentals. Connections provide a path for forces to flow through material. Often, the check for a reasonable solution can be as simple as building a paper model. The need for tape could imply a need for angles or bolts; or additional folds or cardboard could imply mixing in more rigid materials.

As previously mentioned, connections are specific to material. A wood joint has different design goals than a steel connection. These foundations can help designers invent joints for speculative materials in a more engaging way. This is also an opportunity to visually demonstrate the weight and scale of the building. Introducing smaller elements to a large, otherwise flat surface can provide context for a viewer to use as scale. It can also give the viewer a way to get to know more about how the pieces of the puzzle came together. Cleverly depicting ways for materials to come together doesn't need to stray far from the built environment to be interesting and dynamic.

> *For example, if a beam and a column are coming together... with wood construction, the height of the beam may be taller than the width. You may be worried that the beam will tip to the left or right and just get crushed when it falls out of plane and drop everything it was carrying. You'd probably put a collar on the column to support it laterally every once in a while. It would be incredibly rare to see something like that happen on a concrete to concrete connection. Much like a sharp pencil through paper, columns can punch through plates if they don't have enough bearing surface at point of contact. This would be a surprising detail for steel, which is too expensive to transfer weight through sheer mass. Steel will most likely be lighter weight frames welded together to transfer loads.*

Compression is when force flows with gravity. Post and beam connections leverage this. Forces are lowest when efficiently sent directly downward, parallel to gravity. Introducing jogs or diverting this line compounds another vector to the existing downward force. Stacking material is a great way to ensure that these forces stay in-plane. It also minimizes the opportunity for a connection failure by relying on the material itself to be the point of bearing. There's usually some "glue" to keep alignment in check. For wood, this glue is nailed in place, concrete is supported with more concrete, and steel is welded.

There are three types of metal connections varying in flexibility: pinned, shear, and moment. Pinned connections allow for a good amount of movement. In contrast, shear connections provide flexibility such that movement will not cause any pieces to snap. Moment frames are completely rigid and afford no flexibility, for this reason they undergo additional oversight and inspection.

Other than live load and dead load, structural engineers design details to accommodate a variety of different forces:

Tension: The joint is at risk of pulling apart based on the loads going through the bearing members. In these scenarios we see threaded rods and screws being used.

Torsion: If a member is taller than it is wide, or otherwise runs the risk of overturning the type of joint can help with this. Brackets, plates, and kicks are used to stabilize and less responsibility falls solely on the individual fasteners.

Shear: When normal forces are out of plane, increased surface areas help improve the effectiveness of a joint. Increasing the number of connections helps make the most out of surface area overlap and strengthens the wall or framing member.

Columns provide support at a point, using caps or beams to spread out their tributary area. If not large enough, like a pencil through a pencil, it can punch through the surface it is supporting. This is not to say a design cannot taper at the top of a column, there may need to be a cap or reinforcement in order to distribute the upward force. Columns, as with any portion of architecture, can be used as a canvas for decoration or ornament. As you are most likely familiar, columns are a major part of classical architecture. The classical orders have permeated modern styles and ornamentation.

The classical orders are as follows: Tuscan, Doric, Ionic, Corinthian, and Composite as shown in Figure 10.1. Each celebrates a Pediment, Shaft, Capital, Entablature, and Architrave. Above that are the Frieze, Architrave, and Cornice. Each type is designed to three systems of proportions all relating to the diameter of the shaft. The first system is the height of the shaft, from there the height of the column and entablature can be solved. The height of the column with its entablature informs the height of the base, shaft, and entablature.

Tuscan columns are simple and are the most squat, being seven times as tall as they are wide. Doric columns are simple but articulated with shallow flutes around the shaft. Their entablatures are often ornamented with triglyphs and metopes. They are eight times as tall as they are wide. Ionic columns introduce volutes into the capital resembling a scroll. They are nine times a tall as they are wide. Corinthian and composite columns are the most ornate and are both ten times as tall as they are wide. The capitals can depict acanthus leaves, an egg and dart pattern, beams and reels, flames, and lotuses. Composite columns differ from Corinthians minorly with their emphasis on volutes as their own standalone element.

Aside from the classical order, there are a wide variety of column types. Caryatids are literally just female sculptures used as pillars or columns supporting loads. These started as columns for Greek temples but ended up also being employed as supports for fireplaces. They symbolically depicted traits of the deity the temple was meant to serve. Solomonic columns are helical columns that can take on any of the classical capitals. Bernini sculpted a

FIGURE 10.1
Classical Orders of Support Columns

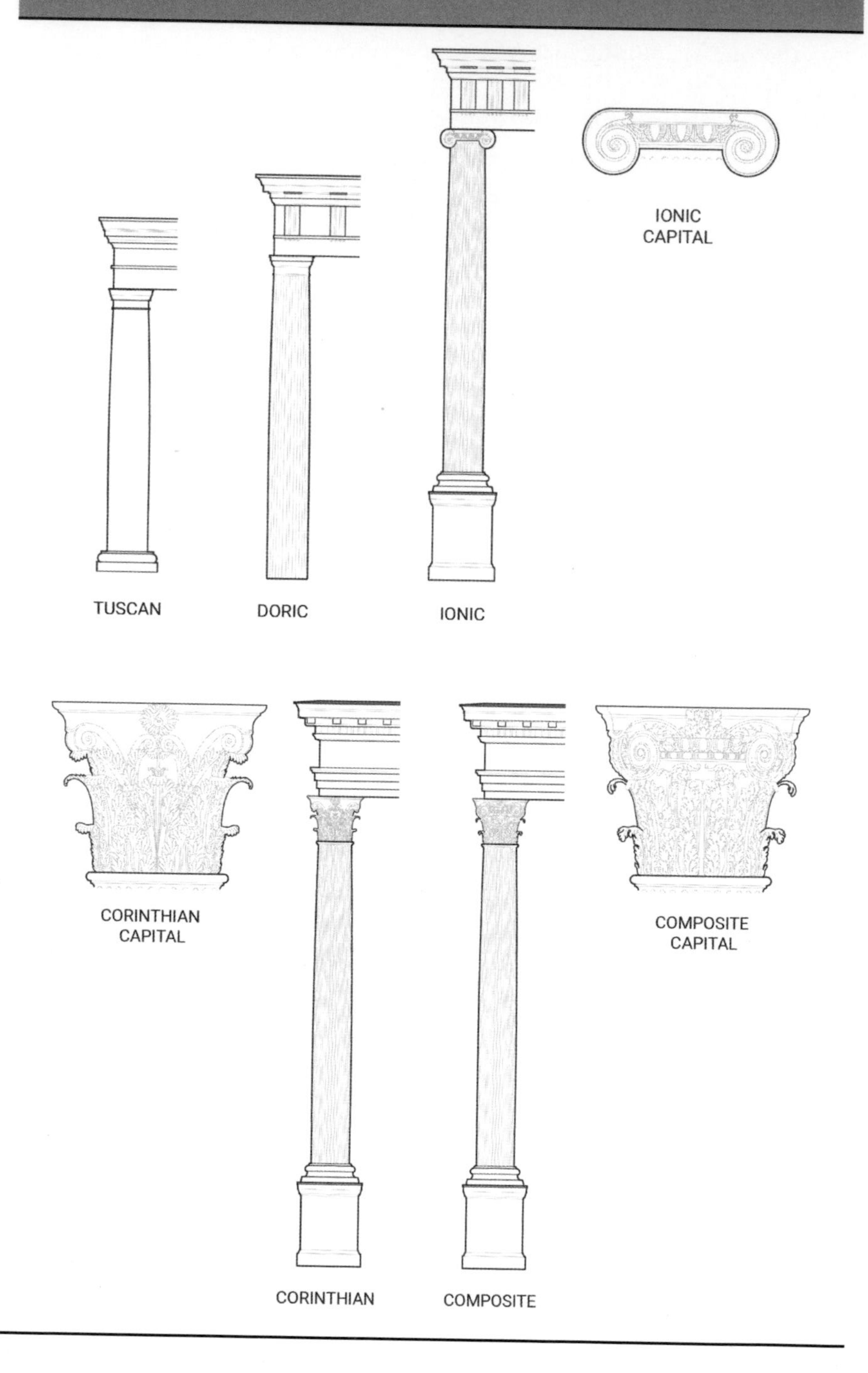

bronze baldachin, with an ornate canopy and solomonic columns, over the altar of St. Peter's Basilica.

Engaged columns are fairly common in modern facades. They can maintain a round cross section or have a square cross section. At Michelangelo's Laurentian Library, columns and their accoutrements were paired in twos and, out of necessity, were engaged in the wall. This was celebrated and challenged at corners where cornices practically melt into each other. Villa Maeria also uses multiple adjacent columns. Playfully depicting multiple understandings of what an extruded point could mean, ranging from a series of vertical columns, forming a screened wall, to a single column. They also varied in ornamentation, clad in either paint, rattan (rope), or wood slats. Mies, thrilled with the opportunities made available by steel, had developed a cruciform column. Corbusier used slender round columns and referred to them as "piloti."

More practical profiles of columns find square or circular cross sections. Concrete columns can have sharp or chamfered edges to prevent cracking and chipping. Columns on exterior walls can leverage an asymmetrical corbel to marry into a beam or provide a sill for floors to bear on in compression rather than shear. Rectangular columns work really well as a termination point for a wall. When standing alone, circular columns can be used in place of rectangular columns to reduce the profile slightly on the diagonal. Steel columns can be wide flanges, hollow squares, hollow tubes, or filled with concrete. Exposed steel is typically painted with intumescent paint which makes it flame resistant. Timber columns are also flame resistant at a certain dimension. Almost none of these is articulated with a pediment or capital. They typically will terminate in a drop cap or thickened slab if there is any articulation of the cap.

Beams share qualities with modern columns, with unique hardware and connection points. As they can work in shear (if they end on a wall or the side of a column) or compression (if they land on ledge or the top of a column), their articulation can vary. In sheer, they'll typically rely on bolts or welds, in compression, the connection can be uncelebrated or articulated with a U-shaped metal bracket. Anchor bolts and plates can be concealed in the center of wood beams. Steel wide flanges will typically use L-shaped brackets mounted to the web of the beam. Concrete columns typically rely on rebar and corbels to prevent movement at joints.

Cantilevers are structural elements supported on one side. Extra long cantilevers can rely on trusses, backspanning, or angled supports. In wood construction, 4–5 feet is an acceptable distance to go without support, concrete construction can go up to 8 feet, steel construction can go longer depending on its available backspan. Some materials offer the ability to taper edges in an effort to reduce weight at the furthest distance from the support.

Suspended structures are often designed to be flexible. Most structures in general afford a swaying movement. This reduces the impact of a seismic event. As suspended structures are more prone to force differentials, especially as their anchor points may encounter different forces, flexibility is important. Cables afford this ability as they work in tension and allow for movement without breaking. As a result, joints must also selectively afford flexibility. Rings and eyelet anchor bolts afford movement without compromising strength.

Guts

As with every section, this one comes with the caveat that your virtual building does not need this to be successful. Because these are mostly hidden in modern architecture, utilities are largely expected to be working in the background. In places with less infrastructure and planning, integration with these utilities is more visible. The concealment of these systems is largely a luxury provided by manufacturing. As you may suspect, modern architecture is incredibly reliant on machines. Air conditioning, plumbing, sprinklers, electricity, are all require mechanical equipment.

If you learn nothing else from this chapter, I want to, at least, clear up the myth that humans can usually travel through vents or sewer access points. This is more than often not the case, but again that doesn't make for the best story and now it's kind of a pop-culture given. Most buildings do have machine rooms and rooftop equipment though! Facilities management and maintenance teams must treat the building like a living machine, they require have more moving parts than many designers care to admit.

Frank Lloyd Wright was one of the first architects to consider the opportunity available in designing the ventilation systems of a building. In the Larkin Building, the air conditioning is embedded in the columns, following the same parti as the rest of the building.

> Control *mimics this in its mailroom, pneumatic tubes mimics the Johnson Wax columns inside a Larkin building style massing. This harkens back to the original open office layout instilling a system of control and lack of privacy.*

Modern structures sequester machine rooms to the basement and top of the building. They cluster them together in low visibility spaces near garages, basements, alleys. Some equipment requires interaction with utilities, like water control rooms, transformer vaults, and gas meters. Smaller buildings can either host these outside or outside of the property line. Elevators require pits below the hoistway and machine rooms above the hoistway. This encourages the concept of a "core" grouping together the systems in the building that need to run from the roof to the basement.

There are a variety of ways air conditioning in a building can work. In order for it to work, it needs access to outside air and the environment that it is intended to cool. Typically the lowest cost air conditioning comes from window units. These are visible from inside and outside of the building. These are often typically tenant supplied solutions for apartments. Packaged terminal air conditioner (PTAC) units are larger and installed in an exterior wall. These are also visible from the inside and outside. Typically used in motels and hotels. Ductless split units, as the name suggests, splits up the outside machine from the inside machine, connecting them with tubes. This allows the outdoor unit to be in a less visible location than the facade. Central air relies on heating, ventilation, and air conditioning (HVAC) units typically on the roof of the building. These allow for some efficiencies like heat recovery but also suffer from temperature loss over distance. Ice storage air conditioning is extremely rare and definitely the coolest one. The concept is that electricity is less expensive during off-peak hours and that can be used to super cool water into a massive ice cube. It slowly melts during the day, cold air is pumped through the building, and the ice cube reforms at night. I have only been in one ice storage cooled building, most of the people working there were unaware.

Heat can come from resistance, heat pumps, steam, or furnaces. The major concept here is similar to air conditioning. As far as mediums go, air is pretty bad at maintaining temperatures, water is pretty great. Electrical resistance heating is wildly inefficient but could make sense if electricity is inexpensive to make. Gas powered equipment is really good at generating heat but require a duct to get exhaust air out of the building.

Ducts that are designed to be visible typically have a round spiral cross section but can have any profile. Supply diffusers, or vents, coming off of them may be directed downward or out. The ducts are usually insulated from the inside and don't need to visually show a puffy "jacket" around them.

Ornament

Ornament in architecture has the opportunity to visually depict cultural values. Typically, like material choices, location and scale of ornament can be functional. These choices can also highlight properties of materials that are particularly relevant to the parti. Adolf Loos drew sharp attention to the lack of necessity or modern function of ornament. Manufactured material allow for clean edges and transitions. Minimalism led to an honest try to explore what architecture could survive without. As it turns out, it reduces the budget as well. If choosing between an ornate building or a larger building, many owners and developers chose the latter. Unless specifically requested by a municipality or if restoring a historic building ornamental detailing will not be entertained.

Often, the client is a person who represents more money than they are personally responsible for. As a result, there are more people approving decisions now than before. Default will prevail and the path of least resistance will direct the design. All of those things considered support the lack of revivals of these more intricate styles. It is not flexible for reduction of scope or scale of cost. That being said, when labor was inexpensive ornamentation it was incredibly prevalent.

Ornament often portrays ideals of the time. Zeitgeist or concepts "of the time." Ornamentation allow for an illustrative depiction of a motif. Functionally providing a pridge between the highly restrained language of architecture and the collective consciousness of the time. The acanthus leaves symbolically represent immortality, adorning a stone building with this is fitting. The building will outlive its owner, designer, and creators—relatively speaking it is immortal. This leaf actually persists through a variety of styles, demonstrating values and key features of that expression. The particulars can be expanded upon by the infinitely many decisions related to the visualization of the leaf. This adds more authorship and opens the sculpture up for interpretation. While the meaning may be straightforward, the relationship to the theme can shine through the nuances of the depiction.

Baroque architecture is known for its elaborate ornamentation. The owner wanted to demonstrate wealth and sophistication through craftsmanship. Characterized by its symmetry and plasticity, baroque ornamentation and forms often praised the church or monarchs. As baroque became more popular, a more playful antithesis evolved. Rococo sought a wider vocabulary, depicting myths and leveraging asymmetry. Rococo also employed pastel colors, white, and gold.

Diablo 3's *Imperial Palace depicts gilded guard rails and flooring accents. They also leverage curves to make spaces seem more voluptuous. A pulpit sits in the center of a carved out space, visually reminiscent of a pulpit from a catholic church. Choosing to do this not only serves as a good solution to a similar problem, drawing attention to and exalting the speaker, but also alludes to a time when organized religion was visually characterized by the inequality of the church and the patrons.*

Modern ornament does exist, despite its 1920s banishment. It does not adorn buildings along seams, but creates a field condition. Modern building materials facilitate patterning with mass fabrication of precise parts.

David Adjaye consistently leverages ornament in 2D and extruded 2D, affectionately dubbed 2.5D. His African American History Museum uses a digitally fabricated wood panel to adorn the building. The milled panels depict an abstraction of handworked wood.

Few modern materials allow for handmade customizations. Most are prefabricated or have a factory finish. Brick is one of the few materials that still holds it traditional ornamentation. Soldier courses functionally host weeps and provide a visual termination to a swath of wall. Though bricks are starting to transition to panelized or slim bricks, reducing the role of a mason on site.

Many instances of modern ornamentation are evenly arrayed or parametrically designed if they do have variation. The designer can delegate some authorship to geometry or logic.

11

Composition

Hierarchy functions as a series of visuals shortcuts to quickly understand articulations as dominant or subordinate. Breaking down a facade can start like an eye exam, is it more or less prominent? How about the next line you see? Is that more or less prominent? Patterns can become visual communication tools to help viewers accurately break down and understand how a building works. Interesting, informative, and compelling textures are created as a result of construction materials or structural constraints. In the absence of those, virtual architecture is tasked with the authorship of these systems to a much more intentional capacity. Functionally composition can help accentuate design choices that are already employed. Meaningful contributions to character through massing choices work even better when accentuated with details of a matching motif.

Functionally, the first recognizable order visually breaks a space into groups, either indicating a part of a whole or a microcosm within the whole. The organization or structure could either respect or deviate from the original, respectively.

> *In* Breath of the Wild, *Hyrule Castle uses scale of room hierarchically. Functionally, scale indicates importance to the main quest. The most challenging fights occur in taller rooms, including the final boss battle. Abstractly, it represents a culturally important piece of architecture. Codifying the environments in this way allows players to determine the importance of a room. This allows players to make decisions on whether or not to invest time in entering. This also gives agency to the player as they're deciding whether to progress the story or not. It also functions as a visual pay-off. This type of hierarchy happens out of necessity in the built environment, which may be why it works well as a narrative device. Rooms are typically "appropriately" scaled because overbuilding costs money and buildings are already expensive. Spaces that are either oversized for the function or excessively tall draw*

attention. Leveraging a trope that many humans subconsciously notice in the built environment is a great way to provide information to your player.

Hierarchy is most often used to indicate priority. If there are certain parts of the design that need to be read as a group, encapsulate that area. Hierarchy can create ambiguity allow for a more complex relationship between rooms or spaces. While not everyone will get the same understanding that the designer intends, it may make an impression or affect the perception of the occupant.

Hierarchy

Developing a hierarchy affords opportunities to solve problems uniquely. Hierarchy gives designers the freedom to choose when to depart from a pattern. It's challenging to create a framework which can house every condition introduced in a project. Revisiting patterns and relying on relationships other than adjacency can help build a rich texture. Hierarchy can be loud, designer should be wary about cacophony if too many portions are competing at the same level. And ultimately, the designer must trust the work to stand on its own, creating a tailored impression as intended.

Hierarchy can be used to indicate use of spaces behind the facade. Inherently, structural constraints related to room size or height will be a major factor in window placement. Providing breaks or segments in the pattern allow for this change to function as a piece of the puzzle. In the example of Notre Dame, we can see that the facade is a nine-square grid, lacking the middle top piece. The emphasis of the engaged columns creates a reading of cohesion of vertical lines over horizontal. Furthermore we see the symmetry of the towers about the centerline of the center form.

Classical buildings and Renaissance buildings both rely heavily on hierarchy. Many resulting styles like Rococo, Neoclassical, and modern buildings adopt the rule, pursuing it with different techniques. Hierarchy can be demonstrated by using 2D and 3D elements, including shadows and material seams. These features can fade in severity with the importance of each layer.

Creating this pattern allows for a more relatable scale, seeming more pleasant or reasonably sized. By providing every window, door, and floor at the same level of importance, the viewer may have less attention span to break down what they're seeing. Forgoing any organizational method may result in an overwhelming or bland building. Controlling the order in which occupants perceive information also helps create more intentional scenes in spaces. Focus is entirely at the agency of the occupant, but can be persuaded or distracted to visually break it down in a certain order as shown below.

Notre Dame leverages arch profiles and slender windows to develop patterns within each square of the nine-square grid as shown below, left. Window profiles can hold integrity despite a variety of proportions addressing individual rooms as shown below, right.

Organizational structures at different scales provide specific understanding at each. This opens up the opportunity to create larger narratives. Buildings have a unique capacity to create a large pattern using smaller elements. The smaller elements can become relatable when demonstrated at more accessible heights. They can distort depth perception as they stretch further away from the viewer/occupant.

The concept of an "antithesis" relates to any discourse with a lineage. Supposing an alternative or opposing standpoint creates new solutions to a similar problem. The rebellion against hierarchy was explored by postmodernists. Fascinated by the opportunity for infinity, architects used grids to symbolize a lack of beginning and end (Superstudio, Archizoom). Paper architects supposed a variety of interesting, but ineffective designs for the building materials of the time. Eisenman and Gehry had completed projects at the cost of functionality, suffering from leaking windows. This also reflects the ideals of the age. Postwar culture fueled cultures like postmodernism. Stagnation or a lack of momentum also spurs a deviation from the status quo. This demonstrates quality through the means of undermining existing "knowns."

Typically, towers will have heavier structure at the base as shown below. Cornices help the building gracefully provide a parapet, where the walls extend past the rooftop, and a cap flashing to prevent water from infiltrating the cladding. These are constraints that most buildings must address with additional material in these areas.

Once the base and tower are visually separated, they are free to individually articulate the function of the space behind the facade. To start, a door and a window have different visual properties, one only occurs at the base of the building or balconies. Windows occur more frequently. By dividing the windows into narrower forms, the building can look much taller as it is composed of smaller vertical shapes. These are constraints of buildings, a virtual building, as indicated by postmodernist thinkers, does not need to follow these rules of thumb.

Directionality can have a major impact on a tower facade without overwhelming it. Compare the following, tower without articulation and one with vertical striations both shown on the next page. The latter should look just a bit taller than former, as shown below.

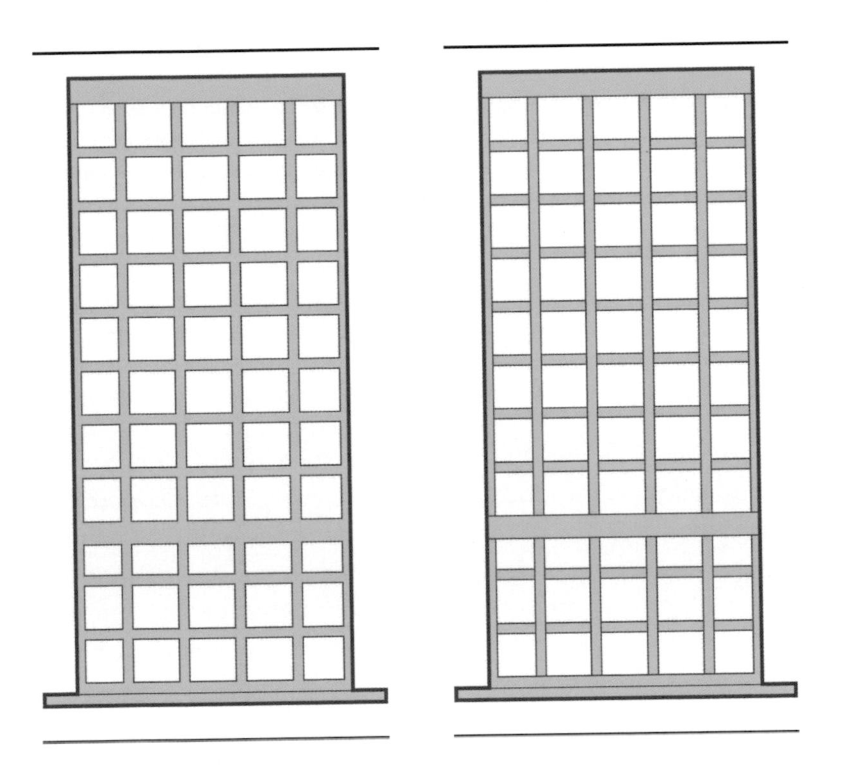

> *The Lever House has two primary masses, of similar proportions at different scales and orientations. The podium or lower portion primes the importance of the horizontality of the tower. The primary face becomes the slab articulated by long horizontal lines. The other opportunity for this building of course would have been to accentuate the verticality tower by rotating the banding to match the relationship established with the lower slab. The fact of the matter is that it aligns with the way the floors actually work in the tower. It visually describes its functionality and holds the details true through the entire tower. While any of the decisions could have made sense, only one version of the design can be built.*

Hierarchy can also tell your player what to focus on or manipulate their first impressions of the building.

> Fallout 3 *features a particularly squat skyscraper, Tenpenny Tower. The new Willard Hotel that it draws inspiration from is actually block building. As a result of this, motifs which weigh a building down made their way into this tower's design. Surface articulations like horizontal banding were inherited. Also, this hotel as built is massive compared to its neighbors. The city probably had restrictions on how tall a building on that plot of land could be. the existing structure is very courteous as it gives some room back to the intersection by chamfering a corner. Tenpenny Tower also takes on this form, but in its new context, doesn't contribute a lot to its character and in some ways undermines it. Tenpenny Tower timidly approaching the edge of its footprint.. We also don't see anything which could depict another side of Tenpenny outside of his dialogue. Something like strong 90 degree corners could imply a rigid unchanging nature as he is greeted with the wasteland but refuses to adapt.*

Graphic designers hold visual communication paramount. Grids are used to align related information and create a structure. Signs are designed to help clarify directions, organization, or some kind of information. Communicating organization of unfamiliar information is a critical role of the designer.

Sizes and typefaces are also used to communicate that information has the same level of importance. If you see a list of lecturers or orchestral performances for a season, everyone has the same scale and typeface. Alternatively, less formal concerts where success is a measurable benchmark for performers, you will see typefaces scale down for lower profile acts and the headliner starts the page with large text. Often the breakdown of hierarchy will be functionally driven in order to create an intuitive experience. Correlations can be drawn between items in a row or column; from there, remnants of those items can make their way into discrete portions of the design. Graphic designers rely heavily on this to help introduce new information to viewers, ordered with intention. The same rules apply to architectural design, collinear or centered items can start to create patterns. Rows and columns can become comparable, commenting on each other with rhythms and patterns.

In *Hyper Light Drifter,* we see spaces organized to indicate a very important feature, using piers and monuments. Smaller areas work in a nine-square grid around it, using cardinal directions for circulation in and out. This allows the significance of that area as a recurring feature to read with the first time the player is introduced to the area. The scale of spaces allows for the player to rank the importance as it relates to the main quest, smaller avenues indicate a portion of the puzzle, larger areas indicate travel to and from main quest areas.

Gorogoa features hierarchical puzzles. Patterns and scales are intentionally subverted in order to challenge the perception of each element. The expectation holds one answer: the ability for the player to abstract the image holds another. By retaining the concept of original function as it relates to the new location allows a more complete story to emerge. The importance of nonlinear storytelling created a requirement for a structure which allowed for visual and haptic correlation between otherwise disparate parts of a story to hold importance, simulating a dream-like organization to the story.

Demonstrating the effects of age or time passing can be done with patina but also with retrofits or counter intuitive solutions. Residents, codes, and cultures change over time, a keen eye can spot the ways to portray it with architecture.

> *Portal 2* leverages a wide variety of building additions to give the areas which aren't test chambers an increased narrative capacity. The corporation as a client pulls the design in a variety of ways which give some background to the intent of research and development. Often in corporate design, a committee will act to represent the mission statement and visualize it. Portal 2 visualizes the transition from a sole owner of a corporation. Later testing areas demonstrates a moment of candor transitioning to a more curated and professional environment.

Uniformity is a recent addition to the conversation, interestingly enough. With the dawn of modernism transitioning to paper architecture, designers questioned the requirement for anything and everything. As a result, it's revealed that a lack of hierarchy becomes increasingly problematic in the pursuit of truly eliminating it.

Patterns

If hierarchy depicts elements working together to tell a story, a dichotomy leverages how elements contrast each other. Using the conceptual negative space, what is missing or expected, a more nuanced understanding can become apparent. For instance, saying that a neighborhood is safe despite having low walls and no bars on windows. As surveyed, security appears to not be present, in reality it may just not be a design feature.

We'll look at three different ways to use contrasting elements in environments. Ranging from large to small, it can be curated by developing a rhythm to set the stage for a contrasting element. At an individual building scale, it can diagram two opposing styles, focusing on the shared goals. As an applied effect, it can be the way light primes players for a dramatic or relaxing moment. The goal of these is to exaggerate the difference between two distinct elements or attributes of the design to call attention to them. Often we'll see this as mixing and matching design goals. It can start with a given or a simple understanding of something and composing a subject or single exception. Another way to set this up is to identify the benefits available through composing styles that may otherwise be at odds.

> *In* Portal, *we see a stark contrast between the test chambers and the mechanical spaces at Aperture Science. Primarily, one could see this as an allegory depicting corporation with a clean outward facing persona showing cracks in the facade. Using the stark contrast to demonstrate perception versus reality expands into finishes and aging. The player is able to compare the two and develop their own perception of events. This gives the player enough information to generate an impression as opposed to being told what to think.*

As previously mentioned, architecture relies heavily on exerting some control over the order in which the occupant notices or perceives information. The concept of subject and field asks the viewer to review two pieces of information at once, putting some priority to one over the other. In this sense, the subject is like the playable area in a parallax game, the field is like the background. The subject should be understandable and quick to breakdown visually. The field can be more abstract and complex. The two together can have a more complex still relationship, based on the breadcrumbs laid down by the more obvious canvases.

Subject and Field

The concept of a field condition on a facade originally began as a material texture. Modern ornament has shifted focus from locational solutions to full building or face solutions procedurally generated geometry. Debord's remarks on knowledge and the development of "the thought of the spectacle" ring eerie parallels to our modern comfort with numerically focused design systems. While these inherently are easier to fabricate, they run the very real risk of becoming divorced from societal nuances. Parametrically designed features can easily turn authorship over to the program or algorithm responsible for creating the design.

When referring to a texture or pattern created on a plane, it is often called a "field." In contrast is the subject—an object that defies the existing pattern. This can refer to a map, a facade, a graphic. Often the contrast between the two will draw attention to their similarities and differences.

For instance, punching a large hole in a facade that is otherwise a grid similar to the style of Steven Holl's Linked Hybrid. Both openings have a relationship to their border, but the open portion of the building leverages a wrapping facade to indicate the primary difference. The opportunity for the small opening to relate to the big opening is not mimicked but is also not foreign.

> *The field can be used to support the subject,* Donkey Kong Country *uses the background to foreshadow hazards and demonstrate the type of environment you can expect to navigate. Inside uses the backgrounds to provide context to the task the player is asked to perform. When experimenting with powers in a shed, the task seems harmless. When experimenting with powers in a controlled lab environment, the task seems suspicious. When busting out of a tank and destroying a building, the task seems powerful. These fields can change the player experience by assisting gameplay or provoking thought.*

Duplicity

There are few tools that can imply "equal" meaning to two different interpretations of an idea. Duplicity in architecture implies that two separate readings can have relevance simultaneously. The simplest implementation is Gestalt. Gestalt's theory is often perceived as "optical illusion." While one image is perceived in advance of the other, the ambiguity grants equal weight to both. The mechanic relies on the solid and void providing enough abstraction to entertain a second look.

This is simple to understand in logos, FedEx has an arrow. It's significance is indicated by a color change in the last two letters. Logo designers leverage this to tell as much as possible with the least amount of articulation. So how does this relate to architecture? It starts with figure/ground and asks the occupant to go a bit further. Once the figure and context are identified, comparing the orientation, arrangement, contrast, allows the opportunity for interpretation. That's the best—that's what makes people feel like they're experiencing something authentic. Gameplay actually helps provide hints for different frames for the player to try on when observing or perceiving the environment. The source material for the mechanic can also manifest in the environment in subtle ways. This could help sync up the intended use with the way the player feels they "should" use a mechanic.

The Vitra Furniture Museum by MVRDV looks like a bunch of monopoly houses got stacked. They latch into each other like Lincoln logs. So the profile of that extruded shape is the pictogram of a house. This is illuminated and holds attention as a figure. The extrusion itself actually looks like a factory. These two readings together allow for the site to hold weight in the interpretation of the structure. The correlation between factory and showroom as well as the relationship of domestic home to furniture on display are both valid readings of the building.

Inside leverages this as the interaction between foreground and background matter deeply. The act of playing the character without knowing why or what you're doing becomes part of the commentary on the setting. The primary difference is that the game takes a somewhat forward approach to this problem by slowly divulging the plot.

12

Affectations in Architecture

An immersive environment can guide occupant behavior and attitude. The most simple example is the way places of worship strive to give occupants the feeling of "awe." Requesting patrons to be reverent and respectful. Sound has an incredibly high reverberation rate, drawing attention to the speaker and allowing their words to linger for just a moment longer. Ceilings, walls, floors all hold ornament and contribute to the transformation of place. Symbols and statues are celebrated by niches carved into walls, framed by the building itself. Relying on everything from the smallest details to the massing of the space to contribute to the concept is incredibly important to create an impactful space. A key part of getting this to work is the variety of materials involved in telling the story. As you know by now, materials have different traits built up over thousands of years of use. Another consideration is that materials may not be able to carry the same type of ornamentation. A pleasant side effect of this is that each must be considered individually and does not lull the viewer into thinking they understand it simply by identifying it. Variation supports finding a common theme through multiple sources, in the way that play is introduced to language. Relying on tangential relationships to provide the occupant with clues to project meaning toward.

A primary difference between built and virtual architecture is the concept of safety. Built structures primarily must resolve safety concerns, virtual environments may opt in to look believable but is not responsible for it. Prospect and refuge are not typical terms in codifying built spaces. "Public" and "private" spaces more accurately describe distinctions between spaces. That being said, there are certainly ways to make a space more comforting than others. Ranging from massing to wall finishes, there are plenty of opportunities to help a player feel "safe." For instance, using curved walls and reducing blind corners can reduce triggers in occupants suffering from Post-Traumatic Stress Disorder (PTSD). Removing doors from closets can help reduce stress in a patient suffering from memory loss. Cool colors can calm, bright colors can inspire.

Leveraging the environment to close the gap between the character's feelings and the player's. For example, introducing a player to a game. Tutorials can be the most immersion breaking moment in a game. The character and player are at opposite ends of the spectrum, presumably the character has been running and jumping for years. The player is being asked for the very first time in this moment.

Empowering the player to feel as if they are inventing or choosing play styles based on context clues makes gameplay moments memorable. Humans are great at comparing two side by side visuals whereas relying on them to be able to compare areas seen in sequence may be less reliable. If two areas need to have a narrative tie to each other, showing them impact or impose on one another will have much more impact than even showing them in succession.

Additionally, creating combat spaces has an exterior challenge. The player is more often than not combat trained. The game supposes that they will know what to do with a supposedly combat trained character certainly with the ability to sail through any and all of the challenges thrown at them. Giving them visibility and visual control over a situation helps bridge this gap. Mystery novels and movies are often told from a single point of view. This builds suspense about plot, "what will happen next." Omniscient point of view (the reader finds out snippets from each character) is used to help the reader put together the facts just a bit faster than the characters do. This builds suspense waiting for characters to react to something the reader already knows. In order to preserve the concept that the character is already a combatant, to some extent, the player needs a bit of upper hand in order to make the character move and act like one would expect a skilled person to. Especially in third person, it's very easy to look silly when you can't master a level or don't know what to do. Sure there are tongue-in-cheek things you can do to break the fourth wall and apologize for the character's behavior. Alternatively, we've seen the camera or UI used to keep the player one step ahead of the characters. In *Doom*, you're given a map to aid this, it's not incredibly effective but is necessary for giving the player omni. In XCom you're given an isometric view. In Halo you're given a heads-up display in your helmet. All of these give a boost of situational awareness to the player in order to make the character "look cool" in combat. The massing of the level can also help this.

These correlations also help in staging combat areas. Incentivizing movement around an area leads to engaging and challenging combat. By using sight lines and space separation, players will naturally need to shift from one space to another. Sequencing vulnerable and desirable spaces in succession creates a desire for progression. Allowing for balanced gameplay can be challenging, but identifying massing opportunities early can allow for balance to be integrated as polish is added.

Notably, the mindfulness of a gesture is critical to the reception of a move. Importance is then held to the control and restraint of the environment's effect on its occupants. Intentionally calling attention to moments around the building and creating an atmosphere can be observed actively and passively. Virtual architecture can achieve this distinction as well.

Priming

Often, directors will telegraph actions to the audience to provide the correct amount of "shock." The viewer shouldn't miss it or need to watch it again to understand. In order to assist with this, the camera can be used to frame a shot, a familiar item can return in a new context. "Chekhov's Gun" famously refers to the expectation that the director will leverage props in this way of foreshadowing. Games can do this as well, providing visual ornamentation that scales from a key to its door or neighborhood-specific outfits for entourage. This can also be something as simple as setting up a staged interaction that provides an additional sight line to a consequential reaction. When using architecture specifically, this can mean leading into a large room with a smaller space to contrast the difference. Going straight into a large room from an outdoor environment actually doesn't give as big of an impact if there's no gasket to reset the player to "indoor" dimensions first.

Developing a system for building expectations for geometry can help build expectations for the player reaction. Leveraging narrative time, games can showcase the same geometry, proportions, or ornament to give the player familiarity with environments. This can also set players up to expect certain interactions. Using spaces to frame expectations can help reduce reliance on dialogue and special effects to ready players for an upcoming encounter. More modern games are experimenting with giving the player some agency during what could otherwise be considered a cut scene, rendering it in the engine. This requires a transition to specific focus or risks a distracted player, moving the camera about while missing crucial information.

Immersion

Driving an environment with atmosphere can help a player have a memorable experience. Contributors can be visuals that play into peripherals, like connecting multiple spaces through sight lines. It can also be creaky floorboards or echoes in large spaces. The goal is to simply provide secondary and tertiary features of a space in support of the visuals. Building the space in this way allows the space to become more complex without introducing distractions.

Architects consider these contributions "phenomenal." They enrich the choices that are already made and work with the existing palette to trigger additional senses. In this segment, we'll focus on forced perspective, context, coordination with other effects, and furniture used to make an environment more encompassing. Using these individually or in tandem heightens the opportunity for the player to be affected by the story. This can be used to provide "proof" or context for comments made through dialogue. If a location is supposed to look abandoned, it can suffer water damage or look dusty. If it is supposed to look cheap, flooring can be lazily installed lacking trim in areas or the ceiling grid can be off-center. Consider how furniture and props can be slightly customized per environment. Being aware of the time spent in spaces and scale the level of detail to match. The concept of a gesamtkunstwerk considers the architect as creator and curator of a complete environment, creating a "complete work of art." (Figure 12.1)

FIGURE 12.1
Phenomenal Transparency

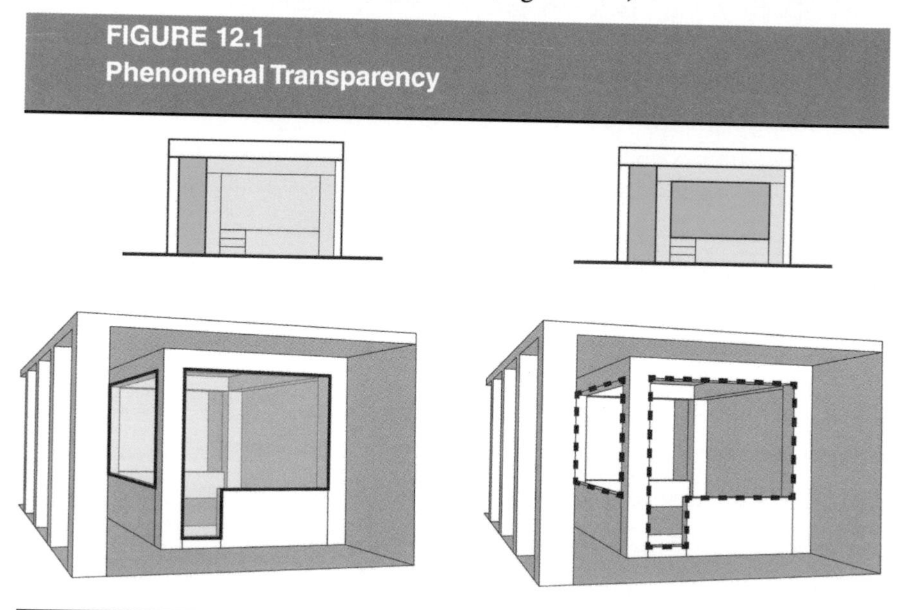

FIGURE 12.2
Shallow Narrowing of Spaces

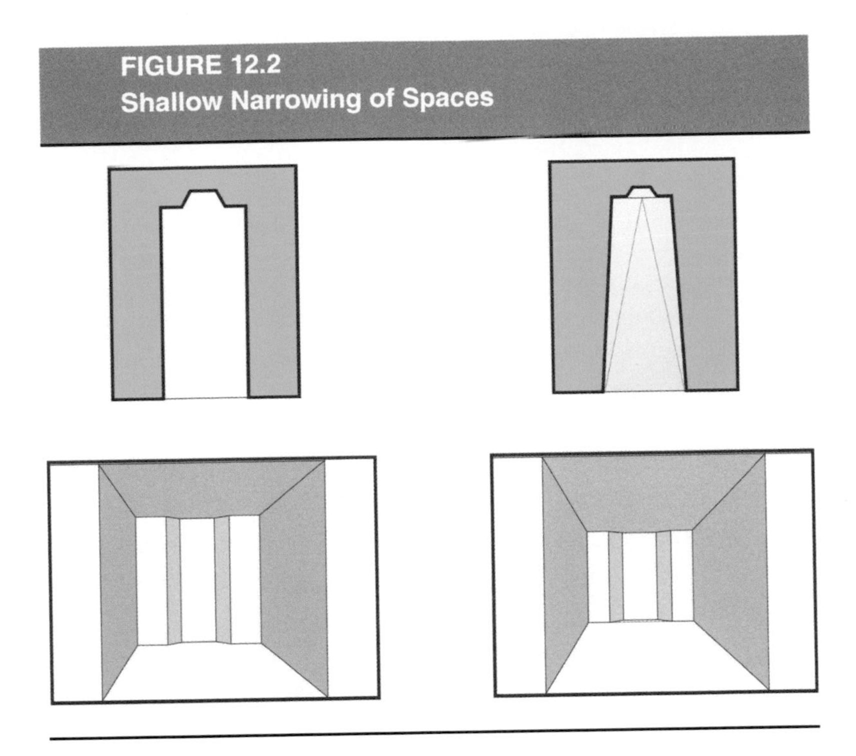

Shallow Narrowing of Spaces is shown in Figure 12.2.

Design tactics employed in theme parks and movie sets often rely on understanding the collective consciousness. This more or less breaks down to the decision point which asks "will the audience get it or be confused?" When overcorrected, it appears as pandering or unoriginal; when not considered, it can be disorienting. Often if you mention another movie or book to set up the elevator pitch, the team is leaning a bit too far on collective consciousness. If it feels like everything is coming out of thin air, the breadcrumbs aren't there for the audience.

Portal and its sequel also rely on gameplay with gradually increasing complexity. The first few puzzles scale from one solution to multiple as the player gains more agency as the character. Using colored light and iconography, the players will gravitate toward certain areas predictably. The grid also provides a burdensome backdrop for each of the test chambers. And those gridlines you see really tap into the idea of modular furniture being primarily consumed as "oppressive." Modular materials are most classically used in large spaces with no particular interest in "hospitality" and notably do not tap into fond memories. DMV's are riddled with these types of materials for instance. These inherent thought processes allow *Portal* to snap the player into the character's mindset of "escape." As a result, the Glados and Wheatley dialogue doesn't tell you what to do or how to feel. This results in an organic and authentic experience for the player, given the opportunity to graft their own thoughts onto the canvas as well.

Drama

To evoke certain emotions, architecture must become reliant on support from lighting, props, and camera angles. Creating a tension for dramatic scenes can be as simple as placing a different colored light at decision points. at this point, architecture becomes a machine for perceiving emotions. Architecture can bind together less tangible or noticeable mediums to work cohesively. Sound design can pick up a change in flooring material with foot falls. It can also pick up a change in lighting with a crackle. Lighting colors can contribute to perception of spaces. Props can provide snippets of stories.

All of that being said, architectural drama is created by height, walls rotating out of "normal," and sequencing of spaces as shown below.

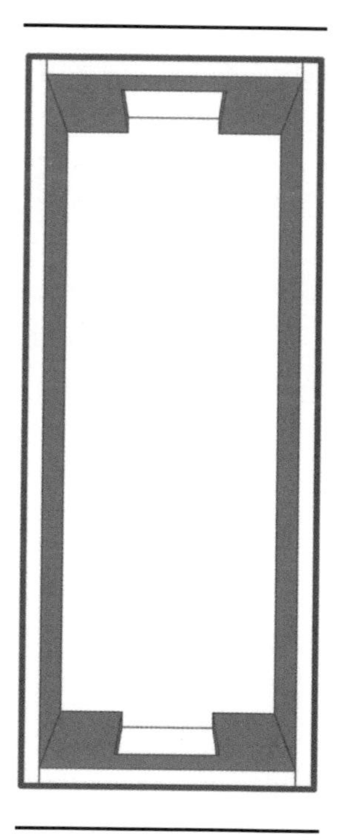

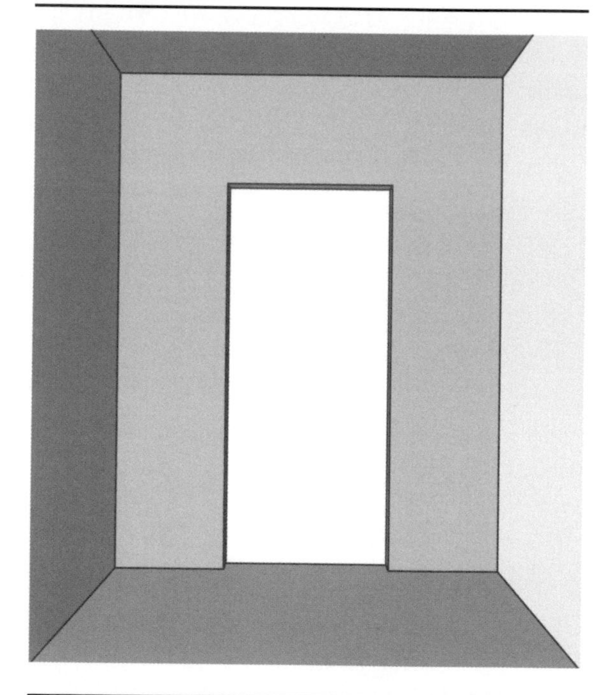

Rotating walls inward makes a space seem closed as shown below.

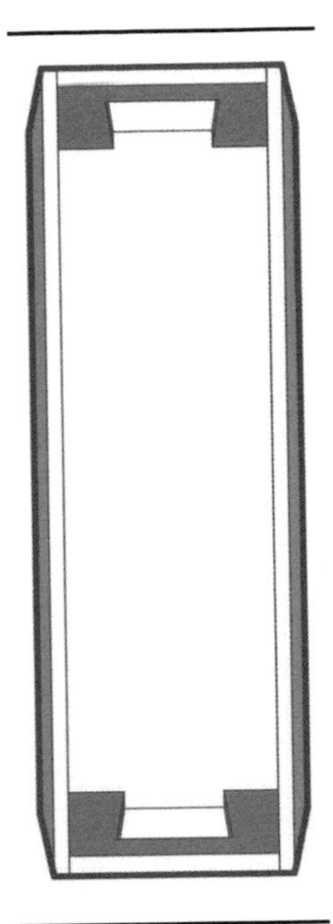

Rotating them outward provides a feeling of relief as shown below.

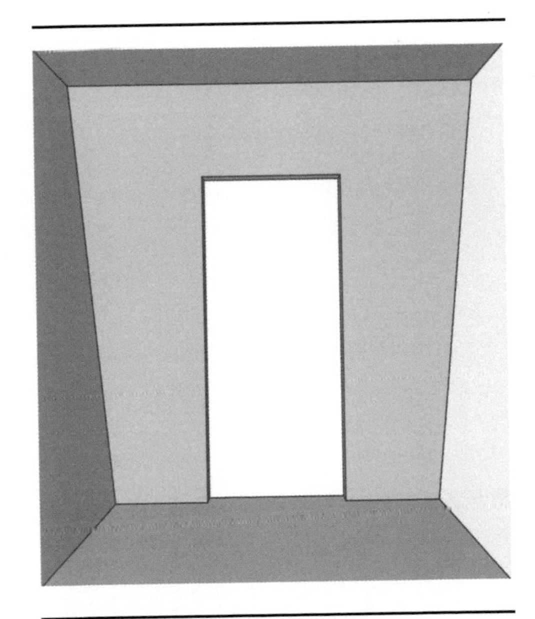

Proximity of architectural elements and scale are the primary ways for humans to determine how large something is at a distance. Roman temples use this to appear larger in subtle ways. The Parthenon leverages continuous columns to connect the ground level to the architrave to establish scale. It also exploits that continuity by tapering the columns as they get further away from the ground. This is called "entasis" and can be found in many eras of architecture.

Spaces can work together when sight lines are established and maintained. Providing transparency to staged spaces can build tension shown on the previous page. The choice to use a translucent barrier (literal transparency) or a framed opening (phenomenal transparency) can also change the way the focal point is perceived. Gardens often use phenomenal as a way of breaking down spaces without using walls. *Bioshock* uses both literal and phenomenal transparency to introduce two enemies with this type of framing. A fairly common enemy, the splicer, is the first enemy you meet. A piece of glass separates you at first but is almost immediately removed. This sets up the expectation that you will encounter the enemy and maybe not on your own terms. The next instance, you see a big daddy kill a splicer from behind glass. The glass stays in place, and sure enough the game often sets the player up to deal with the big daddies on their own terms.

Though space may not be in short supply, travel time can be valuable. Forcing perspectiveas shown earlier in the chapter can also add drama to a scene without changing its scale. Altering the angle of planes, directing them inward at the end of a hallway, can make the hallway seem longer. The limitations are bound to camera type and game style. For instance, this may be more challenging to implement in virtual reality games and could cause spatial discrepancy problems by introducing a ramp.

Interaction

An environment that inspires creative problem solving can come in a variety of forms. Depending on the input from the player, the environment can suggest a sort of incompleteness. Waiting for modification or input from the player. Designing a space to imply a void or rhythm is challenging to the extent that the player must acknowledge the architectural form as malleable, or even at all. Where many architectural design moves work passively as a backdrop, requesting creative input becomes conscious and active for the player. Lighting, color change, arrangement of props, camera angle changes, or simulation graphics can aid in notifying the player.

Visualizing the space that allows play and interaction also requires some finesse.

In many cases the solution starts with a world that is not monolithic. Articulating surfaces with seams or modular pieces can remind the player that the building has flexibility in form. Eroding a corner can demonstrate a lack of rigidity and an openness to change. Demonstrating a logical understanding or organization to the environment creates a collaborative environment. Patterns that demonstrate a game can be played in the medium work very well as starting points for additions or customization. Alternatively, a grid overlay or blank canvas can imply organization. Revealing tiles and modules gives the player agency to create more complicated solutions.

> Portal *leverages this to assist planning, but is still completely devoid of the playfulness that other creative games may have. The game requires creative problem solving on-demand and the articulation of the space visually supports this.*

Eroding or diminishing an edge can be a reminder or clue that this structure could be manipulated. Introducing asymmetry or dynamic elements affords some opportunity to collaborate with what exists already. A highly symmetrical or otherwise resolved composition is much more challenging to contribute to. It may require a break or separation to create additions.

Conclusion

Built and virtual architecture observe different constraints and freedoms. As a result, they need not mimic one another to move forward. While both provide a boundary, the responsibility to the primary objective impacts decisions large and small. Architecture is highly logical for the most part and can often attribute its texture and complexity to the constraints it must face.

If attempting to reach believability through accuracy, one may compromise opportunities to adhere to narrative or gameplay. Creating a true-to-life piece of architecture may have diminishing returns as there are countless pieces that don't have a physical impact on what presumably would be playable spaces. Identifying the details and nuances that evoke feelings that play to the narrative could be a much more effective design tool.

Finding built solutions to a proposed constraint could lead to a more compelling collection of details and textures. Architecture is often defined by the way it gracefully overcomes or avoids constructability challenges. This may mean supposing a smaller pattern to tile in the same way that built structures are often adorned with cladding sized such that a human could install it.

Consider the way the virtual space could have been built. This could lead to support or ancillary spaces that make the environment more believable. As built structures get closer to realization, they must address construction, feasibility, and safety concerns. This forces minor complexities into the design that in an ideal world may not exist. At the same time, it inspires clever solutions and demands texture.

Designing virtual architecture to encompass every aspect of built architecture does not allow the medium to reach its fullest potential. Virtual architect may find inspiration through built structures, but also machines, biology, geology, music. Virtual architecture has the opportunity to maintain rigor and precision relating to narrative and storytelling.

Works Cited

Alexander, Christopher. *A Pattern Language*. Oxford University Press, 1977.

Allen, Edward, and Joseph Iano. *Fundamentals of Building Construction: Materials and Methods*. John Wiley & Sons, 2009.

Allen, Edward, and Patrick Rand. *Architectural Detailing: Function, Constructibility, Aesthetics*. John Wiley & Sons, 2016.
Arnheim, Rudolf. *Film as Art*. University of California Press, 2003.
Arnheim, Rudolf. *The Dynamics of Architectural Form*. University of California Press, 2009.
Bellard, Miriam. "Environment Design as Spatial Cinematography: Theory and Practice." GDC. Game Developers Conference 2019, San Fransisco, CA.
Bogost, Ian. *How to Do Things with Videogames*. University of Minnesota Press, 2011.
Ching, Francis D. K. *Architecture Form, Space and Order*. John Wiley & Sons, 1996.
Ching, Francis D. K. *Building Codes Illustrated: A Guide to Understanding the 2018 International Building Code*. John Wiley & Sons, 2018.
Clark, Roger H. and Michael Pause. *Precedents in Architecture Analytic Diagrams, Formative Ideas, and Partis*. John Wiley & Sons, 2012.
"Composition in Level Design." *LEVEL*, level-design.org/?page_id=2274.
Corbusier, Le, and Frederick Etchells. *Towards a New Architecture*. Butterworth Architecture, 1993.
Debord, Guy. *Society of the Spectacle*. Black & Red, 2010.
Frampton, Kenneth. *Modern Architecture: Critical History*. Hudson and Hudson, 1992.
Hosking, Claire. "Architecture in Level Design." GDC. Game Developers Conference 2016, San Fransisco, CA.
Jacobs, Jane, and Jason Epstein. *The Death and Life of Great American Cities*. Modern Libray, 2011.
Jencks, Charles, and Karl Kropf. *Theories and Manifestoes of Contemporary Architecture*. Academy, 1997.
Mamurra, Lucius Vitruvius, et al. *The Ten Books on Architecture*. Dover, 1960.
Pepin, Roxanne. "The History of Concrete." *Giatec Scientific Inc*, July 5, 2019, www.giatecscientific.com/education/the-history-of-concrete/
Ramsey, Charles George, et al. *Architectural Graphic Standards*. John Wiley & Sons, 1994.
Rowe, Colin. *The Mathematics of the Ideal Villa and Other Essays*. MIT Press, 2009.
Rowe, Colin, and Fred Koetter. *Collage City*. MIT Press, 1981.
Skolnick, Evan, "Believability." *Video Game Storytelling: What Every Developer Needs to Know about Narrative Techniques*. Watson-Guptill Publications, 2014, pp. 73–91.
Stein, Benjamin, and John Reynolds. *Mechanical and Electrical Equipment for Buildings*. John Wiley & Sons, 2000.
Totten, Christopher W. *An Architectural Approach to Level Design*. CRC Press, 2014.
"Tuscan Order." *Tuscan Order*, buffaloah.com/a/DCTNRY/t/tuscan.html
"Why Diversity in Architecture Matters for Communities and the Bottom Line." *Redshift EN*, October 24, 2017, www.autodesk.com/redshift/diversity-in-architecture/

Index

Note: Locators in *italics* refer to figures.